NO POSTAGE
NECESSARY
IF MAILED
IN THE
UNITED STATES

BUSINESS REPLY MAIL

FIRST CLASS   Permit #8   Riverton, WY 82501

Postage will be paid by:

INTERNATIONAL
Aviation Mechanics Journal

P. O. Box 36
1000 College View Drive
Riverton, Wyoming 82501-0036

SUBSCRIPTION DEPARTMENT

NO POSTAGE
NECESSARY
IF MAILED
IN THE
UNITED STATES

BUSINESS REPLY MAIL

FIRST CLASS   Permit #8   Riverton, WY 82501

Postage will be paid by:

Aviation Maintenance Publishers

P. O. Box 36
1000 College View Drive
Riverton, Wyoming 82501-0036

ORDER NUMBER EA-IAR

AIRCRAFT INSPECTION AND MAINTENANCE RECORDS

AN AVIATION MAINTENANCE PUBLISHERS, INC.
TRAINING MANUAL

By John Enga

AVIATION MAINTENANCE PUBLISHERS

International Standard Book Number 0-89100-094-1
For sale by: Aviation Maintenance Publishers
P.O. Box 36 1000 College View Drive
Riverton, Wyoming 82501-0036
Tel: 1 (800) 443-9250

Aviation Maintenance Publishers, Inc.
1000 College View Drive, Riverton, Wyoming 82501

Table of Contents

PREFACE

This book on *Aircraft Inspection and Maintenance Records* is one of a series of specialized study guides prepared for aviation maintenance personnel to be used with a corresponding 35mm filmstrip and recorded tape cassettes.

This series is part of a programmed learning course developed and produced by the Aviation Maintenance Publishers, Inc. (AMP), one of the largest suppliers of aviation maintenance training materials in the nation. This program is part of a continuing effort to improve the quality of education for aviation mechanics throughout the world.

The purpose of each AMP training series is to provide basic information on the operation and principles of the various aircraft systems and their components.

Specific information on detailed operation procedures should be obtained from the manufacturer through his appropriate maintenance manuals and followed in detail for the best results.

This particular manual on *Aircraft Inspection and Maintenance Records* includes a series of carefully prepared questions and answers to emphasize key elements of the study and to encourage the individual to continually test himself for accuracy and retention as he uses this book. A multiple choice final examination is included to allow you to test your comprehension of the total material.

Some of the words will be new to you. They are defined in the Glossary found at the back of the book.

The validity of any program such as this is enhanced immeasurably by the cooperation shown AMP by recognized experts in the field, and by the willingness of the various manufacturers to share their literature and answer countless questions in the preparation of these programs.

If you have any questions or comments regarding this program, or any of the many other programs offered by AMP, simply contact the Sales Dept., Aviation Maintenance Publishers, P.O. Box 36, Riverton, Wyoming 82501, or call 1-800-443-9250.

INTRODUCTION

Inspection of aircraft will often take up the majority of an aircraft maintenance technician's day. One reason for this is due to a shortage of printed information on how to perform this vital task. As a result, the skills of inspecting an aircraft over the years, have been learned the hard way, on the job. Each individual had to develop his own standards and procedures for performing these vital inspections.

The complexity of general aviation aircraft has dramatically increased through the years, and as a result, the new A&P technician is finding it more and more difficult to learn the skills of inspecting and maintaining aircraft. No longer can he slowly develop an inspection technique. Instead, he must develop a basic inspection procedure almost immediately to be able to go on the job and understand the terminology of an inspection form. He must be aware of the need for a proper set of standards to be used in deciding if the aircraft and its components are airworthy, and must be able to make the proper entries in the maintenance records.

The maintenance records of an aircraft are extremely important to the aircraft owner and the technicians who work on them. These records contain the maintenance history of the aircraft and are used to determine the future maintenance required, and are the key to any professional inspection.

The requirements for the up-keep and use of these maintenance records are contained in the Federal Aviation Regulations and several Advisory Circulars. The terminology used in these publications is often complicated and difficult to interpret, with no standard format used to document the maintenance, inspections, and airworthiness directives. This makes it difficult for a new A&P to determine what maintenance has been performed and how to properly approve the aircraft for return to service.

This special publication, *Aircraft Inspection and Maintenance Records*, is designed to provide a clear and understandable foundation in the basics of aircraft inspections and maintenance records.

This text is designed to describe the inspection of aircraft, from the types of inspections to the detailed procedures required to properly inspect an aircraft. The maintenance record sections of this text describe the responsibility of the owner to maintain the required maintenance entries that are placed in these records.

At the end of each section you will find a number of review questions to help your understanding of the material covered. Answers to these questions will be found at the end of the text. Many of the words in this text will be new to you and you will find these words defined in the Glossary.At the back of the text you will find a final examination to check your understanding of this publication.

SECTION I

Inspections Required on Certificated Aircraft

A. Introduction

The owner or operator of an aircraft is primarily responsible for maintaining the aircraft in an airworthy condition. He must ensure that applicable airworthiness directives and inspections are complied with as required by Federal Aviation Regulations (FARs). In addition, he must have all non-airworthy defects that occur between the inspections repaired before he can fly the airplane.

The owner or operator of an aircraft is responsible for the airworthiness of his aircraft.

The types of inspections required on an aircraft are determined by the requirements of Federal Aviation Regulations and several variable factors such as: the owners or operators type of aircraft, choice of inspection programs, or usage of the aircraft. In some situations, the owner or operator has a choice of several different inspection programs to comply with the airworthiness requirements for his aircraft.

1. General aviation aircraft

The requirements for the inspection of general aviation aircraft are specified in Part 91.169 of the Federal Aviation Regulations. This regulation covers all general aviation aircraft with the exception of large airplanes, turbojet or turbopropeller-powered airplanes or aircraft inspected under some other type of FAA approved inspection program.

FAR Part 91.169 specifies the requirement for inspection of all general aviation aircraft.

Part 91.169 states that no person may operate any aircraft unless, within the preceding or last 12 calendar months, it has had an annual inspection or an inspection for the issuance of an airworthiness certificate. In addition to the requirement for an annual inspection, no person may operate an aircraft carrying any persons (other than a crewmember) for hire, and no person may give flight instruction for hire in an aircraft which that person provides, unless within the last or preceding 100 hours of time in service, it has received an annual inspection, a 100-hour inspection, or an inspection for the issuance of an airworthiness certificate. The 100-hour limitation may be exceeded by not more than 10 hours if necessary to reach a place at which the inspection can be done. However, the time in excess of 100 hours must be deducted from the 100 hour interval in computing the time in service until the next 100-hour inspection.

2. Large or multi-engine turbine powered aircraft

The requirements for the inspections of large general aviation aircraft or multi-engine turbine-powered aircraft operated under Part 91 of the

Federal Aviation Regulations are outlined in FAR Part 91.217. This regulation states that the registered owner or operator must select and use one of the following programs for the inspection of that aircraft.

1. A current inspection program recommended by the manufacturer of the airplane.
2. A continuous airworthiness inspection program that is currently in use by a certificated air carrier using the same type of aircraft.
3. An approved continuous inspection program currently in use by a certificated air travel club using the same type of aircraft.
4. An approved continuous inspection program currently in use by a certificated air charter operator using the same type of aircraft.
5. Any other inspection program established by the owner or operator of that airplane and approved by the FAA.

Upon the selection of the type of inspection program, the operator must identify it in the aircraft maintenance records, and use that selected program for the inspection of the airplane.

Each operator must also include in the selected program the name and address of the person responsible for scheduling the inspections required by the program and provide a copy of that program to the persons performing inspections on the airplane and upon request to the FAA.

Owners and operators of aircraft may choose between five different types of inspection programs. Once a program is chosen, it must identify the selected program in the maintenance records of the aircraft.

3. Air taxi and commuter air carrier

The activity of conducting air commerce by any person, other than an air carrier, of persons or property for *compensation* or *hire* is called an *air taxi* or *air charter* operation and is regulated by Part 135 of the FARs.

The inspection and maintenance required on these aircraft depend on the seating capacity of the aircraft. Aircraft that have a seating capacity of nine or less seats excluding the pilot's seat can be maintained using the annual and 100-hour inspection procedures. If the FAA determines that these procedures are not adequate, the operator must then use an inspection program approved by the FAA for his particular type of aircraft.

The owner also has the option to use an approved inspection program of his own choice if he so desires. This is accomplished by the operator submitting the inspection program to the FAA and having them approve that program for his particular aircraft and type of operation.

These aircraft must also comply with the requirement of FAR 135.421 that sets forth additional maintenance requirements for each aircraft engine, propeller, rotor, and each item of emergency equipment. These additional requirements consist of maintaining, inspecting, overhauling, or replacing of these items in accordance with the manufacturer's recommendation.

Aircraft with 10 or more seats excluding the pilot's seat must be maintained according to the requirements of FAR 135.415, 135.417, 135.423, through 135.443, which will consist of a complete maintenance program for these aircraft.

Operators who use their aircraft for hire are called air taxi operators and are regulated by FAR Par 135. Under this regulation, owners have a choice of inspection programs which must be approved by the FAA.

4. Large aircraft operated under Part 125

Large aircraft not operated in Air Carrier service which have a seating capacity of 20 or more passengers or a maximum payload of 6,000 pounds or more are required to be operated and maintained under Part 125 of the Federal Aviation Regulations.

This regulation requires that the operators of these aircraft have an approved inspection program that may be one of the following:

1. A continuous inspection program which is part of a current airworthiness program approved for use by a certificated Air Carrier.
2. An inspection program currently recommended by the manufacturer of the airplane, engines, propellers, appliances, or survival and emergency equipment.
3. An inspection program developed by the operator and approved by the FAA.

The operators of these aircraft must also develop a general maintenance manual and this manual must contain the following:

1. A description of the maintenance organization when the operator performs its own maintenance.
2. A list of those persons with whom the operator has arranged for the performance of the maintenance.
3. The inspection program to be followed in performing the inspections.
4. The method of performing the inspections.
5. The designation of maintenance items that must be reinspected by a designated person after being accomplished. These are repair items that if improperly repaired could result in a failure, malfunction, or defect that would endanger the safe operation of the aircraft. These are called "Required Inspection Items (RII)."
6. The methods of performing these required inspections.
7. Procedures for reinspecting or "buying back" the work to correct discrepancies found during the inspection phase, a reinspection to make sure that the item is now airworthy.
8. Instructions to prevent any person who performs any items of maintenance to correct discrepancies from also doing a required inspection or buying back of that work.
9. Procedures to ensure that work interruptions do not adversely affect required inspections before the aircraft is released for service.

This manual must be presented to the FAA and accepted prior to the operator being allowed to operate the aircraft. Many corporate or executive operators of these aircraft apply to the FAA for a deviation from these rules of Part 125 and if approved, are allowed to operate these aircraft under the rules of Part 91 as described in the preceding paragraph. The FAA has determined that this would allow an equivalent level of safety for highly qualified operators.

5. Air carrier aircraft

Large aircraft that are used to carry passengers on a regularly scheduled basis, such as the airlines, are called air carrier aircraft and are regulated by Part 121 of the FARs.

The inspections on this aircraft are usually part of a continuous airworthiness program which the commercial operator has had approved by the FAA. This continuous airworthiness program is included in the maintenance manual and the procedures of that manual must be closely followed in maintaining the airworthiness of the aircraft.

B. Altimeter and Static System Inspections

From this point, let's examine a few important system inspections as they relate to the type of flying involved. An inspection of the altimeter and static systems is required on an airplane that is operated in controlled airspace under instrument flight rules. This inspection is required every 24 calendar months. The requirements for the performance and detail of this inspection are found in FAR 91.171 and Appendix E of Part 43 of the FARs.

This inspection can be conducted by the following:

1. The aircraft manufacturer.

2. An instrument repair station with the proper ratings.

3. A certificated airframe mechanic for the static systems only.

4. A certificated repair station with the proper ratings.

C. ATC Transponder Inspections

If a person plans to use an ATC transponder installed in an aircraft, he must ensure that the transponder has been tested and inspected within the preceding 24 calendar months and found to comply with the requirements of Appendix F of Part 43 of the FARs.

Transponders must be tested and inspected every 24 calendar months to comply with FARs.

This inspection may be accomplished by the following:

1. A certificated repair station with the proper ratings.

2. The manufacturer, if the transponder was installed by the manufacturer.

D. Manufacturers Recommended Special Inspection

The manufacturer of an aircraft or engine will often specify that an inspection be performed due to a certain type of situation that has occurred, such as a hard landing or engine overspeed. The procedure and details on this type of inspection are usually found in the service manual, service letters, and service bulletins for that particular type of aircraft or engine. By following the directions and procedures as specified, the airworthiness of the aircraft or engine can be properly determined.

QUESTIONS:

1. Who is primarily responsible for the airworthiness of an aircraft?

2. For how many calendar months is an annual inspection valid?

3. If a 100-hour inspection has been exceeded by 4 hours to get to a location where the inspection can be completed, how many hours will the next inspection interval be?

4. What is the inspection requirement on an individually owned Cessna 150 flown by the owner for personal use?

5. Under what conditions is a static system and altimeter inspection required?

6. How often must a static system and altimeter inspection be performed?

7. If an ATC transponder is installed and used in an aircraft, how often must that transponder be inspected?

SECTION II

Types of Inspections

A. Annual Inspection

The annual inspection is a comprehensive inspection of the complete aircraft that is used to determine the airworthiness of the aircraft at the time of the inspection. In addition to the physical condition of the aircraft, the maintenance records, airworthiness directives, and conformity to the original type certificate or manufacturer's specifications, are also checked.

An annual inspection is required every 12 calendar months on those aircraft that require an annual inspection. The term *12 calendar months* is explained as follows: if an annual inspection is performed on the 4th day of April 1985, the inspection period will be valid until midnight on the 30th day of April 1986. An annual inspection will then be due on the 1st day of May 1986.

Annual inspection are required every 12 calendar months. During this inspection all cowling must be removed and all inspection plates opened.

There are two concepts presently in use in the performance of an annual inspection. The most commonly used concept is combining the necessary service and repair functions with the inspection so that the aircraft is returned to service as airworthy by the inspector. The second concept is that of performing the inspection, and if no unairworthy defects are found, the aircraft is returned to service by the inspector. If unairworthy defects are discovered, the aircraft is not returned to service and declared unairworthy by an appropriate entry in the maintenance records. The owner then has to have the unairworthy defects repaired by appropriately rated mechanics who will return the aircraft to service.

1. Persons authorized to perform and return to service an annual inspection

An annual inspection must be performed and returned to service by one of the following:

1. An authorized inspector.
2. A representive of the manufacturer of an aircraft.
3. Personnel of a certificated repair station approved by the FAA to perform that function, usually the Chief Inspector.

B. 100-Hour Inspection

A 100-hour inspection is a comprehensive inspection of the complete aircraft to determine the airworthiness of the aircraft at the time of the inspection. In addition to the physical condition of the aircraft, the maintenance records, airworthiness directives, and conformity to the original type certificate or manufacturers specification, are also checked.

A 100-hour inspection is required on aircraft that are used for hire and also on aircraft that are used for flight instruction when the aircraft is supplied by the flight instructor or the company the flight instructor represents.

There is *no* difference between the physical scope and detail of the 100-hour and an annual inspection. These basically are the same inspections. The legal differences between the 100-hour and annual inspections are:

1. A 100-hour inspection can be performed and returned to service by a certificated airframe and powerplant mechanic whereas an annual inspection must be performed by certain approved inspectors.

2. An aircraft can be flown for 10 hours after a 100-hour inspection is due to reach a place where the inspection can be performed, but an aircraft can only be flown on a special ferry permit after an annual inspection is overdue.

3. An annual inspection is valid in place of a 100-hour inspection, but a 100-hour inspection cannot take the place of an annual inspection.

C. Progressive Inspection

A progressive inspection is an inspection system designed to break a 100-hour or annual inspection down into small parts, completing each part at a different hourly or calendar time basis. The purpose for using this type of inspection is to keep the aircraft from being out of commission for a long period of time while the complete 100-hour or annual inspection is being performed and keep it in airworthy condition at all times.

The progressive inspection is divided into two basic inspection items which are called *routine inspection items* and *detailed inspection items*. The routine inspection items are defined as visual inspection with no disassembly required to perform. The detailed inspection items are defined as those items requiring a thorough examination and disassembly to perform. For example: the compression check of the engine would be classified as a detailed inspection item. A detailed inspection item could also include the overhaul of a part or system on the aircraft.

The frequency and detail of the progressive inspection shall provide for complete inspection of the aircraft within each 12 calendar months and be consistent with the manufacturer's recommendations, and field service experience, as well as the kind of operation in which the aircraft is engaged. The progressive inspection schedule must ensure that the aircraft is airworthy at all times, and will conform to all applicable aircraft specifications, airworthiness directives, and other approved data.

1. Setting up a progressive inspection

When the registered owner or operator of an aircraft desires to use the progressive inspection system, he must submit a written request to the FAA Flight Standards District Office having jurisdiction over the area in which they are located and shall provide the following:

1. The name of a certificated mechanic holding an inspection authorization, or a certificated repair station, or the manufacturer of the aircraft, to supervise or conduct the progressive inspection.

2. A current inspection procedures manual that is available and readily understandable to the pilots and maintenance personnel containing, in detail, the following:

   a. An explanation of the progressive inspection, including the continuity of inspection responsibility, the making of required reports, and the keeping of records and technical reference material.

   b. An inspection schedule specifying the intervals in hours or days when routine and detailed inspections will be performed including instructions for exceeding an inspection interval by not more than 10 hours while enroute and for changing an inspection interval because of service experience.

   c. Sample routine and detailed inspection forms and instructions for their use.

   d. Sample records and reports and instructions for their use.

3. Enough housing and equipment for the necessary disassembly and proper inspection of the aircraft.

D. Appropriate Current Technical Information For The Aircraft.

The FAA will determine if the proposed inspection procedures will properly maintain the aircraft in an airworthy condition. If the procedures will, the owner will then be given permission to begin the inspection system.

The progressive inspection begins with a complete annual inspection. After this complete inspection, routine and detailed inspections must be conducted as prescribed in the progressive inspection schedule with procedures in the inspection manual being followed.

If the owner of the aircraft decides to discontinue the progressive inspection, he shall immediately notify the local General Aviation District Office in writing that he is discontinuing the progressive inspecton. After this notification, an annual inspection will be due unless the last complete inspection was completed less than 12 calandar months previous. If the last complete inspection was performed less than 12 months ago the annual inspection will be due 12 calendar months from the date of the last complete inspection. A 100-hour inspection will be due within 100 hours of the last complete inspection of the aircraft. The aircraft then reverts back to the annual and 100-hour inspection system.

1. Progressive inspection supervisory requirement

The progressive inspection requires an authorized inspector (or an approved inspector of a certificated repair station) to supervise and make sure that the inspection is being properly conducted. The person responsible for this is named in the inspection manual that is submitted to the FAA.

2. Persons authorized to perform the progressive inspection

The inspection manual for the progressive inspection will include the qualifications of the maintenance personnel that will be authorized to perform the routine and detailed inspection items and return the aircraft to service. A certificated airframe and powerplant mechanic will be able to perform most of the inspection items in a progressive inspection.

E. Approved Inspection Program

An approved inspection program is an inspection system that is agreed upon between the owner and the FAA to ensure the airworthiness of an airplane.

When the owner of an airplane decides to establish and use an inspection program of his own design, he must submit the program for approval to the local General Aviation District Office having jurisdiction over the area in which the airplane is based. This program must include the following information:

1. Instructions and procedures for the conduct of inspections for the particular make and model of airplane, including necessary tests and checks. The instructions and procedures must set forth in detail the parts and areas of the airframe, engines, propellers, and appliances, including emergency equipment required to be inspected.

2. A schedule for the performance of the inspections that must be performed under the program are expressed in terms of time in service, calendar time, number of system operations, or any combination of these.

The local General Aviation District Office will then determine if the inspection program will properly maintain the aircraft in airworthy condition. If it will, they approve the program for that particular airplane.

2. Persons authorized to perform and return to service

The persons authorized to perform and return an aircraft to service after a phase of the inspection is completed can be one of the following:

1. A certificated airframe and powerplant mechanic.

2. Designated personnel of a certificated repair station authorized to perform maintenance on that type of aircraft.

3. The manufacturer of that type of aircraft.

It should be noted that an approved inspection program is considered part of maintenance and must be approved by persons authorized to perform the maintenance and return to service the items on the aircraft in accordance with FAR 43.9 and FAR 43, Appendix A.

F. Conformity Inspection

When an aircraft is designed and built by the manufacturer, its specifications and equipment are approved by the FAA. If any changes or alterations are performed on the design or equipment of the aircraft these alterations must be approved. A conformity inspection is used to determine if any changes or alterations have been made to an aircraft. This inspection is usually an integral part of all aircraft inspection systems as an aircraft cannot be in airworthy condition if there have been any alterations performed on it, or its equipment, without proper approval.

A conformity inspection determines if changes or alterations have been properly made.

The approval for an alteration will be found in an appropriate entry in the maintenance records and returned to service by a certificated mechanic if the alteration is considered a minor alteration. If the alteration is determined to be a major alteration, a Major Repair and Alteration Form (FAA Form 337) must be in the aircraft records describing the alteration, and approved for return to service.

A conformity inspection is also required when an aircraft is to be exported to, or imported from another country. Further, this type of inspection is recommended when performing a *pre-purchase inspection* for a prospective buyer of an aircraft.

QUESTIONS:

1. Who can approve a section of an approved inspection program to service after it has been completed?
2. If an annual inspection is performed on June 6, 1985, when will the inspection expire?
3. Can an annual inspection be signed off as completed in the maintenance records if the aircraft is unairworthy?
4. Who can perform an annual inspection?
5. What aircraft are required to have a 100-hour inspection?
6. Can an aircraft be legally flown if its annual inspection has expired? If so, how?
7. How many hours can a 100-hour inspection be exceeded if it is necessary to fly the aircraft to a place where the inspection can be performed?
8. Who can approve the aircraft for return to service after a 100-hour inspection?
9. What is the primary advantage of using the progressive inspection system for inspecting an aircraft?

SECTION III

Inspection Standards and Procedures

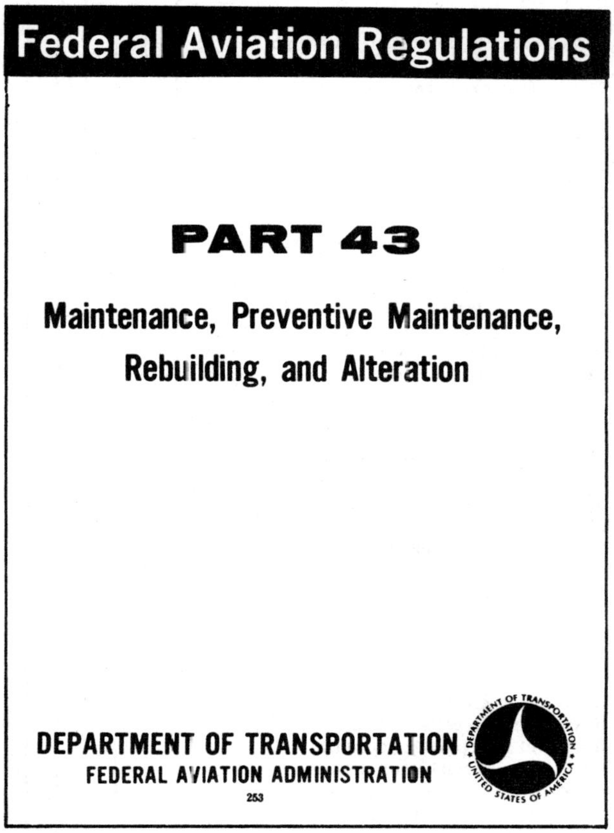
Federal Aviation Regulations

PART 43

Maintenance, Preventive Maintenance, Rebuilding, and Alteration

DEPARTMENT OF TRANSPORTATION
FEDERAL AVIATION ADMINISTRATION
253

FAR Part 43 is the primary reference publication for maintenance personnel.

A. Inspection Performance Standards

The inspection of an aircraft to determine its airworthiness requires a great amount of skill and judgment. For the most part, the items to be inspected are usually listed in a checklist provided by the manufacturer of the aircraft. But, how well an individual inspects an item, or, in what order they are inspected, is up to the inspector. The determination of the airworthiness of an item is up to the judgment of the individual. All of these factors combine together to require the inspector to develop a system or procedure that he can use to effectively inspect an aircraft.

It is essential that an inspector set up a set of standards for himself so he may effectively determine if an item is airworthy. These standards must be high enough to guarantee the airworthiness of the aircraft, and yet, not so high as to cause needless expense for the owner. The inspector must also withstand the pressures that may be applied on him by others to lower his standards and represent items *airworthy* when they are not. Once these standards are compromised, it is very difficult to restore your integrity as an aircraft inspector.

1. Inspection performance rules

Each person performing a 100-hour, annual, or progressive inspection shall perform those inspections in such a manner as to determine whether the aircraft concerned meets all applicable airworthiness requirements. This statement is a part of the FAR 43.15, and means that the aircraft must be physically airworthy, it must conform to its type certificate and manufacturers specification, and comply with all applicable airworthiness directives.

All aircraft being maintained under an approved inspection program must also meet the requirements of FAR 43.13. This states that each person maintaining, or altering, or performing preventive maintenance, shall use methods, techniques, and practices acceptable to the FAA. He shall use the tools, equipment, and test apparatus necessary to assure completion of the work in accordance with accepted industry practices. If special equipment or test apparatus is recommended by the manufacturer involved, he must use that equipment or its equivalent acceptable to the FAA.

a. Checklist requirements

Each person performing an annual or 100-hour inspection must use a checklist while performing

PIPER AIRCRAFT CORPORATION

INSPECTION REPORT

THIS FORM MEETS REQUIREMENTS OF FAR PART 43

Make **PIPER NAVAJO**	Model PA-31 (Turbo) PA-31-300	Serial No.	Registration No.

Circle Type of Inspection (SEE NOTE 1, PAGE 3)
50 100 500 1000 Annual

Perform inspection or operation at each of the inspection intervals as indicated by a circle (◯).

DESCRIPTION	L	R	50	100	500	1000	Inspector
A. PROPELLER GROUP							
1. Inspect spinner and back plate . . .	O	O	O	O	O	O	
2. Inspect blades for nicks and cracks .	O	O	O	O	O	O	
3. Check for grease and oil leaks . . .	O	O	O	O	O	O	
4. Lubricate per lubrication chart. . .	O	O		O	O	O	
5. Check spinner mounting brackets . .	O	O		O	O	O	
6. Check propeller mounting bolts and torque	O	O		O	O	O	
7. Inspect hub parts for cracks and corrosion	O	O		O	O	O	
8. Rotate blades and check for tightness in hub pilot tube	O	O		O	O	O	
9. Check propeller air pressure (Check at least once a month.)	O	O		O	O	O	
10. Check condition of propeller de-icer system, Piper Service Manual, Section XIV	O	O		O	O	O	
11. Remove propellers, remove sludge from propeller and crankshaft . . .	O	O			O	O	
12. Overhaul propeller	O	O				O	
B. ENGINE GROUP							
CAUTION: Ground Magneto Primary Circuit before working on engine.							
1. Remove engine cowl	O	O	O	O	O	O	
2. Clean and check cowling for cracks, distortion, and loose or missing fasteners	O	O		O	O	O	
3. Drain oil sump (SEE NOTE 2, PAGE 3) .	O	O	O	O	O	O	
4. Clean suction oil strainer at oil change (Check strainer for foreign particles.)	O	O	O	O	O	O	
5. Change full flow (cartridge type) oil filter element (Check element for foreign particles.)	O	O	O	O	O	O	
6. Check oil temperature sender unit for leaks and security	O	O		O	O	O	
7. Check oil lines and fittings for leaks, security, chafing, dents and cracks .	O	O		O	O	O	
8. Clean and check oil radiator cooling fins	O	O		O	O	O	
9. Remove and flush oil radiator . . .	O	O			O	O	
10. Fill engine with oil as per lubrication chart	O	O	O	O	O	O	
11. Clean engine	O	O		O	O	O	
12. Check condition of spark plugs (Clean and adjust gap, .015 to .018, as required.)	O	O		O	O	O	
13. Check ignition harnesses and insulators (High tension leakage and continuity.) .	O	O		O	O	O	
14. Check magneto main points for clearance (Set clearance at .016.) . . .	O	O		O	O	O	
15. Check magneto retard points for proper retard angle (37° 30')	O	O		O	O	O	
16. Check magnetos for oil leakage. . .	O	O		O	O	O	

DESCRIPTION	L	R	50	100	500	1000	Inspector
17. Check breaker felts for proper lubrication	O	O		O	O	O	
18. Check distributor blocks for cracks, burned areas or corrosion, and height of contact springs	O	O		O	O	O	
19. Check magnetos to engine timing (20° BTC)	O	O		O	O	O	
20. Overhaul or replace magnetos (SEE NOTE 3, PAGE 3)	O	O		O	O	O	
21. Remove air cleaner screen and clean .	O	O	O	O	O	O	
22. Remove and clean fuel injector inlet line screen (Clean injector nozzles as required.) (Clean with acetone only.) . .	O	O	O	O	O	O	
23. Check condition of alternate air door and box	O	O		O	O	O	
24. Check intake seals for leaks and clamps for tightness	O	O		O	O	O	
25. Inspect condition of flexible fuel lines .	O	O		O	O	O	
26. Replace flexible fuel lines (SEE NOTE 3) .	O	O				O	
27. Check fuel system for leaks	O	O		O	O	O	
28. Check fuel pumps for operation (Engine driven and electric.)	O	O		O	O	O	
29. Overhaul or replace fuel pumps (Engine driven and electric.) (SEE NOTE 3) . .	O	O				O	
30. Replace hydraulic filter element (Check element for contamination.)	O	O		O	O	O	
31. Check hydraulic pump and gasket for leaks	O	O		O	O	O	
32. Overhaul or replace hydraulic pump (SEE NOTE 3)	O	O				O	
33. Check pressure pump and lines . .	O	O		O	O	O	
34. Overhaul or replace pressure pump (SEE NOTE 3)	O	O			O	O	
35. Check throttle, alternate air, injector, mixture and propeller governor controls for travel and operating condition . .	O	O		O	O	O	
36. Check exhaust stacks and gaskets (Replace gaskets as required.) . . .	O	O	O	O	O	O	
37. Check breather tube for obstructions and security	O	O		O	O	O	
38. Check crankcase for cracks, leaks, and security of seam bolts	O	O		O	O	O	
39. Check engine mounts for cracks and loose mounting.	O	O		O	O	O	
40. Check all engine baffles	O	O		O	O	O	
41. Check rubber engine mount bushings for deterioration	O	O		O	O	O	
42. Check firewalls for cracks	O	O		O	O	O	
43. Check firewall seals	O	O		O	O	O	
44. Check condition and tension of alternator drive belt	O	O		O	O	O	
45. Check condition of alternator and starter	O	O		O	O	O	
46. Replace pressure inlet filter . . .	O	O		O	O	O	
47. Replace pressure line filter	O	O			O	O	
48. Lubricate all controls (Do not lubricate Teflon liners of control cables.) . .	O	O		O	O	O	

Owner:

Continued on reverse side

230 211 12/10/68

Circle Type of Inspection (SEE NOTE 1, PAGE 3)
50 100 500 1000 Annual

DESCRIPTION	L	R	50	100	500	1000	Inspector
B. ENGINE GROUP (cont.)							
49. Overhaul or replace propeller governor (SEE NOTE 3, PAGE 3)	○	○				○	
50. Complete overhaul of engine or replace with factory rebuilt (SEE NOTE 3). . . .	○	○				○	
C. TURBOCHARGER GROUP							
1. Visually inspect system for oil leaks, exhaust system leaks and general condition	○	○	○	○	○	○	
2. Inspect the compressor wheel for nicks, cracks or broken blades	○	○		○	○	○	
3. Check for excess bearing drag or wheel rubbing against housing . . .	○	○		○	○	○	
4. Check turbine wheel for broken blades or signs of rubbing	○	○		○	○	○	
5. Check rigging of alternate air control .	○	○		○	○	○	
6. Check oil inlet and outlet ports in center housing for leaks	○	○		○	○	○	
7. Check turbine heat blanket for condition and security	○	○		○	○	○	
8. Check linkage between by-pass valve and actuator	○	○		○	○	○	
9. Inspect induction and exhaust components for worn or damaged areas, loose clamps, cracks and leaks	○	○		○	○	○	
10. Inspect fuel injection nozzle reference manifold for deteriorated hose, loose connections, leaks or obstructions. .	○	○		○	○	○	
11. Check fluid power lines for leaks and security	○	○		○	○	○	
12. Inspect for oil leakage from the controller	○	○		○	○	○	
13. Check operation of compressor by-pass door	○	○		○	○	○	
D. CABIN GROUP							
1. Remove inspection panels				○	○	○	
2. Inspect cabin entrance, door and windows for damage and operation				○	○	○	
3. Check emergency exit latching mechanism .				○	○	○	
4. Check upholstery for tears				○	○	○	
5. Check seats, seat belts, security brackets and bolts				○	○	○	
6. Check trim operation.				○	○	○	
7. Check rudder pedals				○	○	○	
8. Check parking brake				○	○	○	
9. Check control wheels, column, pulleys and cable				○	○	○	
10. Check landing, navigation, cabin and instrument lights.				○	○	○	
11. Check instruments, lines and attachments .				○	○	○	
12. Check gyro operated instruments and electric turn and bank (Overhaul or replace as required.)				○	○	○	
13. Check pitot tube(s), lines and static vents for condition, security and stoppage				○	○	○	
14. Check altimeter (Calibrate altimeter system in accordance with FAR 91.170, if appropriate.)				○	○	○	
15. Change manifold pressure gauge filters . .				○	○	○	
16. Drain crossfeed line				○	○	○	
17. Check operation - fuel selector valve . . .				○	○	○	

Perform inspection or operation at each of the inspection intervals as indicated by a circle (○).

DESCRIPTION	50	100	500	1000	Inspector
18. Check operation - crossfeed valve		○	○	○	
19. Check operation - emergency shut-off valve .		○	○	○	
20. Check operation - heater fuel valve. . . .		○	○	○	
21. Check switches to indicators registering fuel tank quantity		○	○	○	
22. Check condition of heat ducts		○	○	○	
23. Check oxygen outlets for defects and corrosion		○	○	○	
24. Check oxygen system operation and components		○	○	○	
E. FUSELAGE AND EMPENNAGE GROUP					
1. Remove inspection plates and panels . . .		○	○	○	
2. Check baggage door latch and hinges . . .		○	○	○	
3. Check fluid in brake reservoir (Fill as required.)	○	○	○	○	
4. Check battery, box and cables (Check at least every 30 days. Flush box as required and fill per instructions on box.)	○	○	○	○	
5. Check heater for fuel or fume leaks . . .		○	○	○	
6. Check recommended time for overhaul of heater per Piper Service Manual, Section XIII		○	○	○	
7. Check electronic installations		○	○	○	
8. Check bulkheads and stringers for damage .		○	○	○	
9. Check antenna mounts and electric wiring. .		○	○	○	
10. Check hydraulic power pack fluid level (Fill as required.)	○	○	○	○	
11. Check hydraulic power pack and lines for damage and leaks		○	○	○	
12. Check fuel lines, valves and gauges for damage and operation		○	○	○	
13. Check security of all lines		○	○	○	
14. Check vertical fin and rudder surfaces for damage		○	○	○	
15. Check rudder and tab hinges, horns and attachments for damage and operation.		○	○	○	
16. Check vertical fin attachments		○	○	○	
17. Check rudder and tab hinge bolts for excess wear		○	○	○	
18. Check rudder trim mechanism		○	○	○	
19. Check horizontal stabilizer and elevator surfaces for damage		○	○	○	
20. Check elevator and tab hinges, horns and attachments for damage and operation . . .		○	○	○	
21. Check horizontal stabilizer attachments . .		○	○	○	
22. Check elevator and tab hinge bolts and bearings for excess wear		○	○	○	
23. Check elevator trim mechanism.		○	○	○	
24. Check aileron, rudder, elevator and trim cables, turnbuckles, guides and pulleys for safety, damage and operation		○	○	○	
25. Clean and lubricate elevator and rudder trim drum screw.			○	○	
26. Check rotating beacon for security and operation		○	○	○	
27. Lubricate per lubrication chart		○	○	○	
28. Check condition of pneumatic de-icers . . .		○	○	○	
29. Check security of AutoPilot servo bridle cable clamps		○	○	○	
F. WING GROUP					
1. Remove inspection plates and panels . . .		○	○	○	
2. Check surfaces, skins and tips for damage and loose rivets.		○	○	○	

(2)

Circle Type of Inspection (SEE NOTE 1, PAGE 3) 50 100 500 1000 Annual	50	100	500	1000	Inspector
DESCRIPTION					
F. WING GROUP (cont.)					
3. Check ailerons and tab hinges and attachments		O	O	O	
4. Check aileron and trim cables, pulleys and bellcranks for damage and operation		O	O	O	
5. Check aileron balance weight for security		O	O	O	
6. Check flaps and attachments for damage and operations		O	O	O	
7. Inspect condition of bolts used with flap and aileron hinges (Replace as required.)				O	
8. Check all exterior bearings			O	O	
9. Lubricate per lubrication chart	O	O	O	O	
10. Check wing attachment bolts and brackets		O	O	O	
11. Check engine mount attaching structure		O	O	O	
12. Remove, drain and clean fuel filter bowl and screen (Drain and clean at least every 90 days.)	O	O	O	O	
13. Check fuel cells and lines for leaks and water		O	O	O	
14. Fuel tanks marked for capacity		O	O	O	
15. Fuel tanks marked for minimum octane rating		O	O	O	
16. Check fuel cell vents		O	O	O	
17. Check condition of pneumatic de-icers		O	O	O	
G. LANDING GEAR GROUP					
1. Check oleo struts for proper extension (Check for proper fluid level as required.)	O	O	O	O	
2. Check nose gear steering control and travel		O	O	O	
3. Check wheels for alignment		O	O	O	
4. Put airplane on jacks		O	O	O	
5. Check tires for cuts, uneven or excessive wear and slippage		O	O	O	
6. Remove wheels, clean, check and repack bearings		O	O	O	
7. Check wheels for cracks, corrosion and broken bolts		O	O	O	
8. Check tire pressure (N42 - M60)	O	O	O	O	
9. Check brake lining and disc		O	O	O	
10. Check brake backing plates		O	O	O	
11. Check brake and hydraulic lines		O	O	O	
12. Check shimmy dampener		O	O	O	
13. Check gear forks for damage		O	O	O	
14. Check oleo struts for fluid leaks and scoring.		O	O	O	
15. Check gear struts, attachments, torque links, retraction links and bolts for condition and security		O	O	O	
16. Check downlock for operation and adjustment.		O	O	O	

Perform inspection or operation at each of the inspection intervals as indicated by a circle (O).	50	100	500	1000	Inspector
DESCRIPTION					
17. Check torque link bolts and bushings (Rebush as required.)			O	O	
18. Check drag and side brace link bolts (Replace as required.)				O	
19. Check gear doors and attachments		O	O	O	
20. Check warning horn and light for operation		O	O	O	
21. Retract gear - check operation		O	O	O	
22. Retract gear - check doors for clearance and operation		O	O	O	
23. Check anti-retraction system		O	O	O	
24. Check actuating cylinders for leaking and security		O	O	O	
25. Check position indicating switches and electrical leads for security		O	O	O	
26. Lubricate per lubrication chart		O	O	O	
27. Remove airplane from jacks		O	O	O	
H. OPERATIONAL INSPECTION					
1. Check fuel pump, fuel cell selector and cross-feed operation	O	O	O	O	
2. Check fuel quantity and pressure or flow	O	O	O	O	
3. Check oil pressure and temperature	O	O	O	O	
4. Check alternator output	O	O	O	O	
5. Check manifold pressure	O	O	O	O	
6. Check alternate air	O	O	O	O	
7. Check parking brake	O	O	O	O	
8. Check gyro pressure gauge	O	O	O	O	
9. Check gyros for noise and roughness	O	O	O	O	
10. Check cabin heater operation	O	O	O	O	
11. Check magneto switch operation.	O	O	O	O	
12. Check magneto RPM variation	O	O	O	O	
13. Check throttle and mixture operation	O	O	O	O	
14. Check propeller smoothness	O	O	O	O	
15. Check propeller governor action	O	O	O	O	
16. Check electronic equipment operation	O	O	O	O	
I. GENERAL					
1. Aircraft conforms to FAA Specifications	O	O	O	O	
2. All FAA Airworthiness Directives complied with	O	O	O	O	
3. All Manufacturers Service Letters and Bulletins complied with	O	O	O	O	
4. Check for proper flight manual	O	O	O	O	
5. Aircraft papers in proper order.	O	O	O	O	

NOTES:

1. Both the annual and 100 hour inspections are complete inspections of the airplane - identical in scope. Inspections must be accomplished by persons authorized by FAA.
2. Intervals between oil changes can be increased as much as 100% on engines equipped with full flow (cartridge type) oil filters - provided the element is replaced each 50 hours of operation.
3. Replace or overhaul as required or at engine overhaul. (For engine overhaul, refer to Lycoming Service Instructions No. 1009.)

REMARKS:

Signature of Mechanic or Inspector	Certificate No.	Date	Total Time on Airplane

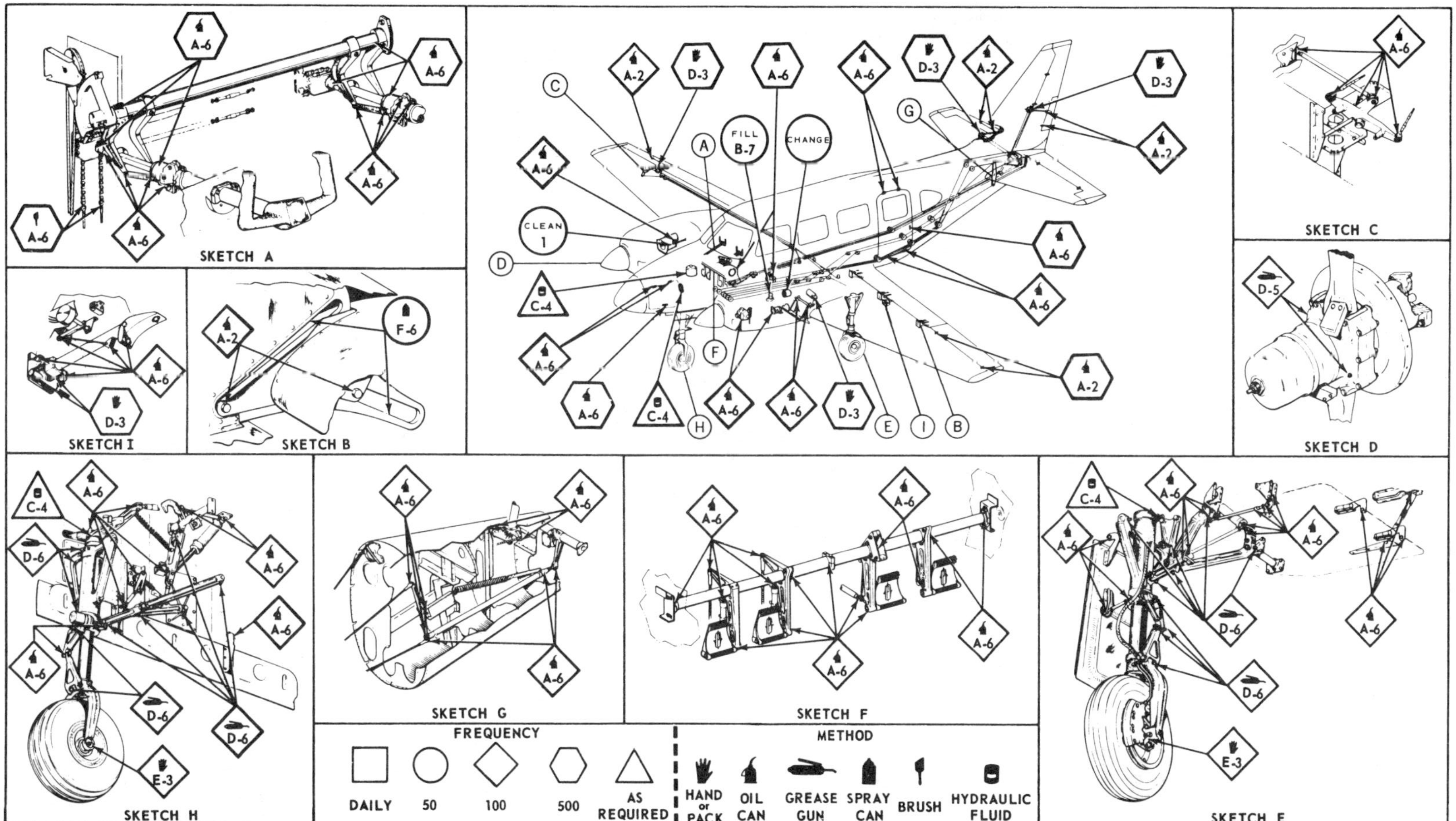

EXAMPLE

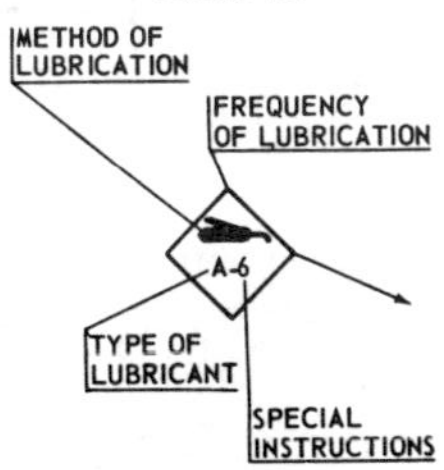

LUBRICATION CHART

TYPE OF LUBRICANTS

IDENTIFICATION LETTER	SPECIFICATION	LUBRICANT
A	MIL-L-7870	LUBRICATING OIL, GENERAL PURPOSE, LOW TEMPERATURE
B	MIL-L-6082	LUBRICATING OIL, AIRCRAFT RECIPROCATING ENGINE (PISTON) GRADE AS SPECIFIED SAE 50 ABOVE 60° F AIR TEMP. SAE 40 30° TO 90° F AIR TEMP. SAE 30 0° TO 70° F AIR TEMP. SAE 20 BELOW 10° F AIR TEMP.
C	MIL-H-5606	HYDRAULIC FLUID, PETROLEUM BASE
D	MIL-G-23827	GREASE, AIRCRAFT AND INSTRUMENT, GEAR AND ACTUATOR SCREW
E	MIL-G-3545	GREASE, AIRCRAFT, HIGH TEMPERATURE
F	---	ALL PURPOSE SLIP SPRAY DUPONT NO. 6611

SPECIAL INSTRUCTIONS

1. AIR FILTER – TO CLEAN FILTER, BLOW OUT WITH COMPRESSED AIR FROM GASKET SIDE OR WASH IN WARM WATER AND MILD DETERGENT, AND DRY. DO NOT USE OIL.
2. BEARINGS AND BUSHINGS – CLEAN EXTERIOR WITH A DRY SOLVENT BEFORE RELUBRICATING.
3. COWL AND FLAP TRANSMISSIONS AND SCREWS, TRIM SCREWS AND WHEEL BEARINGS – DISASSEMBLE AND CLEAN WITH A DRY SOLVENT. WHEN REASSEMBLING TRANSMISSIONS, FILL WITH LUBRICANT AND APPLY A THIN COATING TO SCREW.
4. OLEO STRUTS, POWER PACK RESERVOIR AND BRAKE RESERVOIR – FILL PER INSTRUCTIONS ON UNIT OR CONTAINER, OR REFER TO SERVICE MANUAL, SECTION II.
5. PROPELLER – REMOVE ONE OF THE TWO GREASE FITTINGS FOR EACH BLADE. APPLY GREASE THROUGH FITTING UNTIL FRESH GREASE APPEARS AT HOLE OF REMOVED FITTING.
6. LUBRICATION POINTS – WIPE ALL LUBRICATION POINTS CLEAN OF OLD GREASE, OIL, DIRT, ETC. BEFORE RELUBRICATING.
7. LUBRICATING OIL – INTERVALS BETWEEN OIL CHANGES CAN BE INCREASED AS MUCH AS 100% ON ENGINES EQUIPPED WITH FULL FLOW (CARTRIDGE TYPE) OIL FILTERS – PROVIDED THE ELEMENT IS REPLACED EACH 50 HOURS OF OPERATION.

NOTES

1. PILOT AND PASSENGER SEATS – LUBRICATE TRACK ROLLERS AND STOP PINS AS REQUIRED. (TYPE OF LUBRICANT: "A".)
2. WHEEL BEARINGS REQUIRE CLEANING AND REPACKING AFTER EXPOSURE TO AN ABNORMAL QUANTITY OF WATER.
3. SEE LYCOMING SERVICE INSTRUCTIONS NO. 1014 FOR USE OF DETERGENT OIL.

CAUTIONS

1. DO NOT USE HYDRAULIC FLUID WITH A CASTOR OIL OR ESTER BASE.
2. DO NOT OVER-LUBRICATE COCKPIT CONTROLS.
3. DO NOT APPLY LUBRICANT TO RUBBER PARTS.

680301

an inspection. This checklist may be of the person's own design, one provided by the manufacturer of the equipment being inspected, or one obtained from another source. This checklist must include the scope and detail of the items listed in Appendix D of Part 43 of the FAR. If it is a *rotorcraft* the items that are listed in Paragraph b. of FAR 43.15.

b. Functional checks required

When a 100-hour or annual inspection is completed, and before the aircraft can be returned to service, the engines must be run and checked for the following:

1. Static or full power rpm with the aircraft stationary or not moving.
2. Idle rpm.
3. Magnetos and ignition system.
4. Fuel pressure if equipped with a fuel pressure gauge.
5. Oil pressure.
6. Oil temperature.
7. Cylinder temperature if equipped with a cylinder temperature gauge.
8. All other operating systems for manufacturers' specifications.

After a 100-hour or an annual inspection, functional checks are required before returning an aircraft to service.

c. Rotorcraft performance rules

When performing a 100-hour, annual, or progressive inspection on a rotorcraft the following items are listed as specific inspection items in Paragraph b, of the FAR 43.15.

1. The drive shafts or similar systems.
2. The main rotor transmission gear box for obvious defects.
3. The main rotor and center section (or the equivalent area).
4. The auxiliary rotor on helicopters.

When inspecting rotorcraft, specific inspection items are listed in FAR 43.15.

These items are to be inspected in accordance with the maintenance manual of the manufacturer of the helicopter and must comply with all other inspection requirements of the maintenance manual.

B. Inspection Procedures

The inspection of aircraft requires that the persons performing the inspection organize their work so that the inspection can be performed in a logical and orderly sequence. This will ensure that the aircraft is properly inspected with little chance that any inspection item will be overlooked or forgotten. The accepted method of performing an inspection used by the aircraft maintenance industry, also includes the service and repair activities necessary to return the aircraft to service. Including these activities into the inspection procedure requires that the inspector follow an organized plan in completing the inspection of the aircraft.

The inspection of the aircraft is divided into basically five identifiable phases. They are listed as follows:

1. Pre-inspection phase

The pre-inspection phase begins when the owner of the aircraft requests the services of a shop to perform an inspection on his aircraft. This phase includes completing a work order, research of the maintenance records, airworthiness directives, service bulletins, aircraft cleaning, engine run-up checks (if required), removal of inspection plates, cowling, interior seats, carpets, and upholstery as required. At this point tools and equipment are made ready, and any known parts that will be needed are ordered.

During the "pre-inspection phase" removal of aircraft cowling is necessary.

2. Look phase

The look phase is the actual inspection of the aircraft. It consists of looking at, feeling, checking, measuring, operating, moving, testing, and whatever else is needed to determine the condition of the aircraft and its components. A checklist should be used with a planned sequence or order in which the various items of the aircraft will be inspected.

A method should be used to record the discrepancies and needed service that is discovered during this phase of the inspection. Interrupting the inspection to perform repairs and service should be avoided as much as possible at this point. The necessary repairs and service should be accomplished *after* the complete aircraft and engine has been inspected.

The primary purpose of the look phase is to determine the airworthiness of the aircraft and its components. All of the other activities included in the *inspection of the aircraft* are dependent upon, and in support of, the look phase of the inspection.

3. Service and repair phase

The service and repair phase of the inspection is the necessary maintenance that is required to return the aircraft to service and keep it in airworthy condition until the next inspection. This service consists of lubricating wheel bearings, moving parts, and bearings, replacing and cleaning filters and screens, adding fluids in the brake and hydraulic reservoirs, servicing the battery, and cleaning the aircraft. The repair phase includes replacement, repair, and overhaul of the aircraft components and systems that are in an unairworthy condition.

4. Functional check phase

After maintenance and/or inspection, and before an aircraft can be returned to service, the mechanic should conduct functional or operational checks on the aircraft or systems on which he has worked. Before a 100-hour or annual inspection can be approved for return to service, the person returning the aircraft to service should

During the "look phase" of an inspections, the mechanic looks, feels, checks, measures, operates, and moves whatever is need to determine the physical condition of the aircraft and its components.

run the aircraft engine(s) to determine that they will perform in accordance with the manufacturers recommendations of power output, (static and idle rpm), magnetos, fuel and oil pressure, cylinders and oil temperatures. This is a requirement that is directed by FAR 43.15 which is a minimum functional check required on most engine installations. Additional checks are usually recommended to ensure that *all* of the systems that are installed in a particular aircraft or engine are in airworthy condition according to the manufacturers' specifications.

5. Return to service phase

After an inspection and/or maintenance, and before an aircraft can fly, certain statements,or notations must be made in the maintenance records and signed by the appropriately rated mechanics. This statement, or notation and signature made in the maintenance record is called *approving the aircraft for return to service.*

A typical return to service entry for a 100-hour inspection would consist of the date, aircraft total time in service, a notation describing the maintenance and service performed on the aircraft, and a record of compliance with airworthiness directives and service bulletins. This would be followed by the statement, *"I certify that this aircraft has been inspected in accordance with a 100-hour inspection and was determined to be in airworthy condition".* This statement would be followed by the signature and certificate number of the person returning the aircraft to service. The aircraft can then be legally flown.

In the "functional test phase" a mechanic will often run up the aircraft engine to determine if they meet the manufacturer's recommended performance figures.

QUESTIONS:

1. List three possible sources where a checklist may be acquired or designed for performing an inspection.
2. What does the term *static rpm* mean in performing a functional check?
3. List the functional checks that are required on an engine when completing a 100-hour inspection.
4. List the five phases that make up an inspection program on an aircraft.
5. The actual inspection of the aircraft is called which phase of the inspection program?
6. How do we approve an aircraft for return to service?

SECTION IV

Performing a 100-Hour Inspection

A. *Pre-inspection Preparation*

The 100-hour inspection begins when the owner of an aircraft requests that this inspection be performed on his aircraft. At this time, a *work order* should be completed listing the desired maintenance to be performed and the owner should present the maintenance records on his aircraft. The pre-inspection phase is very important as it serves to organize the work to be performed. This phase will usually include the following steps.

1. *Work order completion*

The work order is the contract between the shop and the owner of the aircraft concerning the work that is to be performed. It lists the work and serves as a record of parts, supplies and manhours of labor that are expended on the aircraft. While interviewing the owner, one should list the work requested and any discrepancies that the owner would like to see repaired. *The owner should then sign the work order before any work is done on the aircraft.*

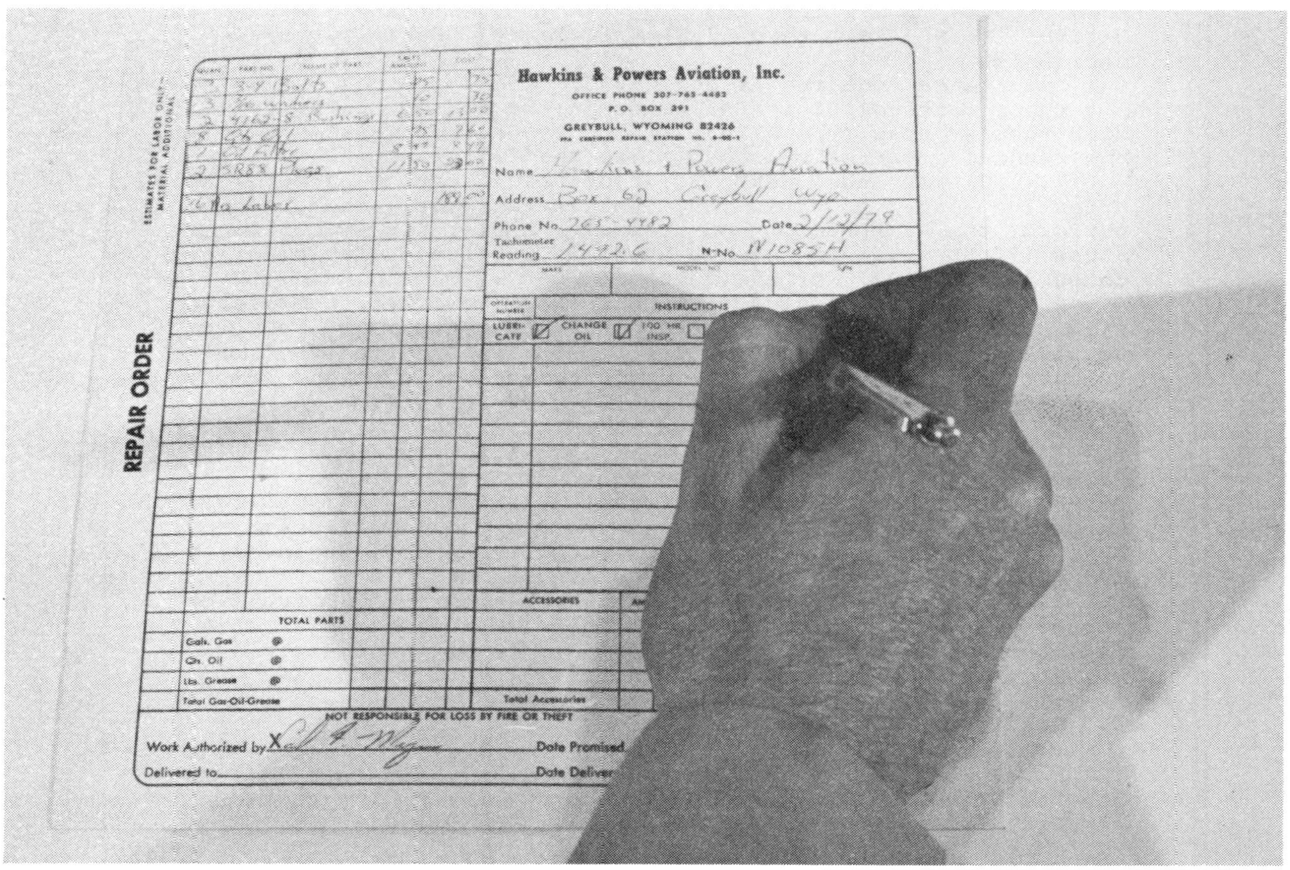

The work order is the "contract" between the shop and the owner of the aircraft and must be completed in detail prior to performing any work on the aircraft.

2. *Maintenance records*

Maintenance records will often tell an inspector a lot about the care and maintenance that an aircraft has had. These records should be researched for information concerning type of oil being used, when spark plugs were last changed, age of the battery, when vacuum system filters were last changed, and engine time since the last overhaul. A very important part of this record research is the notation of compliance with airworthiness directives.

A list of the AD's complied with and the method of compliance should be drawn up for comparison with the AD book for directives that may apply to that aircraft and equipment. A list of the completed service letters and bulletins should also be made.

DEPARTMENT OF TRANSPORTATION
FEDERAL AVIATION ADMINISTRATION
FLIGHT STANDARDS SERVICE
FLIGHT STANDARDS NATIONAL FIELD OFFICE
P O BOX 25082
OKLAHOMA CITY, OKLAHOMA 73125

April 17, 1978

Airworthiness Directive

The following Airworthiness Directive issued by the Federal Aviation Administration in accordance with the provisions of Federal Aviation Regulation, Part 39, applies to an aircraft model of which our records indicate you may be the registered owner. Airworthiness Directives affect aviation safety. They are regulations which require immediate attention. You are cautioned that no person may operate an aircraft to which an Airworthiness Directive applies, except in accordance with the requirements of the Airworthiness Directive (FAR 39.3).

78-08-09 GRUMMAN AMERICAN: Amendment 39-3191. Applies to Models G-164 (S/N 1 thru 400), G-164A (S/N 401 thru 1674), and G-164B (S/N 1B thru 79B) airplanes certified in all categories.

Compliance required as indicated.

To prevent collection of water in the bottom of the rudder main tubular spar (P/N A1203-11) of the rudder assembly and the resulting corrosion, accomplish the following:

1. Within the next 50 hours in service after the effective date of this AD, unless already accomplished, perform the inspection and corrosion protection specified in Steps (1) thru (6) of Grumman American Service Bulletin No. 61 dated June 6, 1977, or equivalent.
2. Within the next 300 hours in service after compliance with paragraph (1) of this AD, and within every 300 hours in service thereafter, visually inspect the exterior of the main tubular spar for corrosion. If corrosion is noted, comply with Steps (5) and (6) of the bulletin or equivalent.
3. If repairs are required in (1) and (2) of this AD, they shall be in accordance with Advisory Circular 43.13-1A, Paragraph 74, Figure 2.7 or equivalent.
4. Upon request, with substantiating data submitted through an FAA Maintenance Inspector, the compliance times specified in this AD may be adjusted by the Chief, Engineering and Manufacturing Branch, FAA, Eastern Region.
5. Equivalent methods of compliance with this AD must be approved by the Chief, Engineering and Manufacturing Branch, FAA, Eastern Region.

This amendment is effective April 21, 1978.

FOR FURTHER INFORMATION CONTACT:

I. Mankuta, Airframe Section, AEA-212, Engineering and Manufacturing Branch, Federal Building, J.F.K. International Airport, Jamaica, New York 11430; Tel. 212-995-2875.

Pictured above is a sample of an airworthiness directive published by the FAA to correct an unsafe condition which may exist on a particular aircraft.

The past maintenance history should be carefuly examined to determine repetitive maintenance problems as well as previous major alterations and repairs that have been performed. All previously performed major alterations or repairs should be carefully examined on the aircraft to see if they have been properly done.

3. Airworthiness directives

Airworthiness directives are issued by the FAA to correct unsafe conditions that may affect the safe flight of an aircraft. Thus, it is important to comply with *all* directives that apply to the aircraft being inspected. To be sure all directives for an airplane are found, the inspector must develop an effective system. A suggested procedure and format is as follows:

1. Use a format similar to the one shown on the next page.

2. Using the AD subject index, list the AD notes on the format that apply to the aircraft, engine, and propeller model involved.

3. Check the appliances and equipment in the aircraft against the AD subject index and record on the format the AD notes that apply to the appliances and equipment installed in the aircraft.

4. Research the applicability part of each AD note listed to see if the model, serial numbers, total time or other criteria can be used to determine if the AD note applies to the aircraft. Note on a worksheet if it applies or does not apply.

It is important to keep all Airworthiness Directives (ADs) on file in a shop library for reference by mechanics. It is also important to keep them in order so ADs on a particular aircraft are easy to locate.

AIRWORTHINESS DIRECTIVE WORK SHEET

AIRCRAFT MAKE: MODEL: SERIAL NUMBER: N NUMBER:

AD Number	Subject	One Time	Recurring	Method of Compliance	Date/ Time C/W	Next Due Date/ time	Applicable	Not Applicable	Remarks

5. Research the maintenance records to see if the AD notes that apply to the aircraft have been complied with, and their method of compliance. Record this information on a worksheet.
6. Determine if AD notes that apply are recurring. If recurring, make a note of it on a worksheet along with the total time or date of the last compliance and when compliance is required next.
7. During inspection of the aircraft, inspect where practical, to determine if compliance with AD notes were made.
8. Comply with all AD notes that apply to the aircraft.

4. Service letters and bulletins

Service letters and bulletins are issued by the manufacturer of an aircraft and may require an inspection to correct unsatisfactory conditions which may exist. The compliance of these letters or bulletins is not mandatory on most small aircraft, but the owner should be encouraged to comply with them.

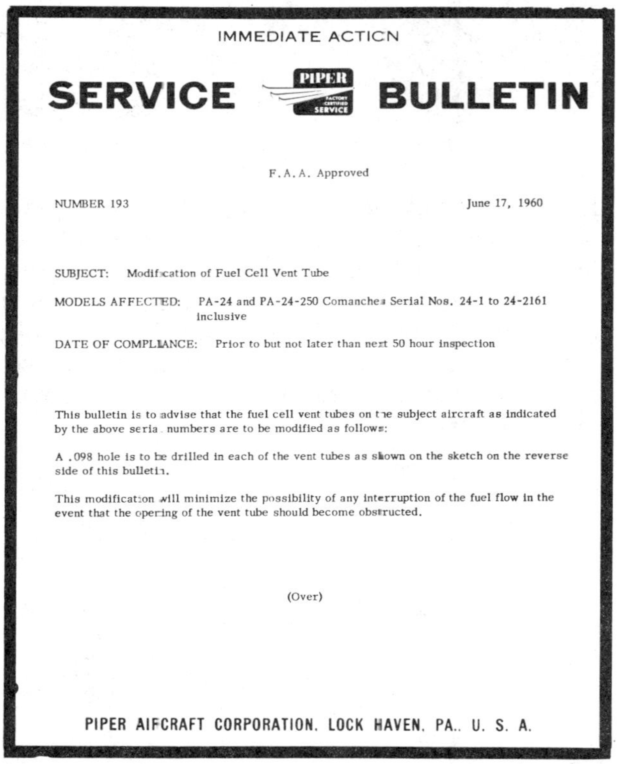

IMMEDIATE ACTION

SERVICE BULLETIN

F.A.A. Approved

NUMBER 193 — June 17, 1960

SUBJECT: Modification of Fuel Cell Vent Tube

MODELS AFFECTED: PA-24 and PA-24-250 Comanches Serial Nos. 24-1 to 24-2161 inclusive

DATE OF COMPLIANCE: Prior to but not later than next 50 hour inspection

This bulletin is to advise that the fuel cell vent tubes on the subject aircraft as indicated by the above serial numbers are to be modified as follows:

A .098 hole is to be drilled in each of the vent tubes as shown on the sketch on the reverse side of this bulletin.

This modification will minimize the possibility of any interruption of the fuel flow in the event that the opening of the vent tube should become obstructed.

(Over)

PIPER AIRCRAFT CORPORATION, LOCK HAVEN, PA., U. S. A.

Service bulletins, issued by aircraft manufacturers, are on unsatisfactory conditions which may exist on a certain aircraft.

Service bulletins and letters are listed according to a year and a number (such as 78-4). This indicates that the bulletin was issued during 1978 and it was the 4th bulletin issued during that year for a particular manufacturer. To determine if a bulletin applies to a particular aircraft, the first step is to check the index of current bulletins that apply to the type and model of aircraft, engine, propeller or appliances. Make a list of these bulletins by type and model. Then check the serial number of the equipment against applicable serial numbers in the contents of the service bulletin. Record those bulletins that apply by the serial number and compare them to the bulletins that have been complied with in the maintenance records. Those that have not been complied with would then be due.

The service bulletins that are due should be discussed with the owner of the aircraft to determine if he desires to comply with them.

5. Aircraft cleaning

The requirement that the aircraft and engine be cleaned before performing the annual or 100-hour inspection is listed in Appendix D of FAR Part 43. Cleaning of the engine and aircraft is necessary so that a proper inspection of the components can be accomplished. If the source of fuel, oil, or hydrualic fluid residue can not be determined, it will be necessary to operate the engine or system before beginning the inspection. A clean engine or aircraft will make the inspection much easier as cracks and discrepancies will not be hidden by the dirt and dust.

6. Parts and equipment required

During the pre-inspection phase, it will become evident that part or kits required by the maintenance record research, service bulletins and airworthiness directives will be needed. These parts should be ordered as soon as possible.

Also, each aircraft will require certain types of special shop equipment such as jacks, stands, hydraulic power supplies, external electrical power, and other test equipment. These should be serviced and placed in the working area as required.

Small tools and equipment needed include a good source of light, an inspection mirror, a 10X magnifying glass and a supply of cleaning towels. These should be available in the working area.

7. Removal of inspection plates and cowlings

Before performing an inspection, it is necessary to remove or open all inspection plates, access doors, fairings, and cowlings, so the inside of the structure and its parts can be inspected. Special care must be taken to keep from losing the screws and plates. Each inspection plate should be marked or identified so that it can be reinstalled the same way at the same location.

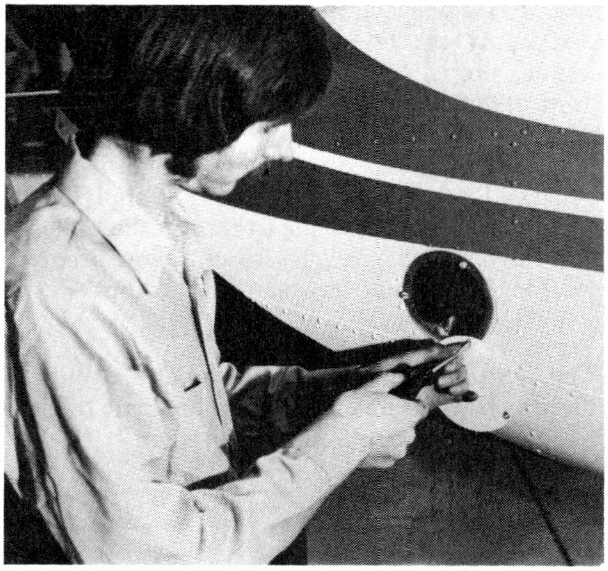

Inspection plates must be removed prior to inspection.

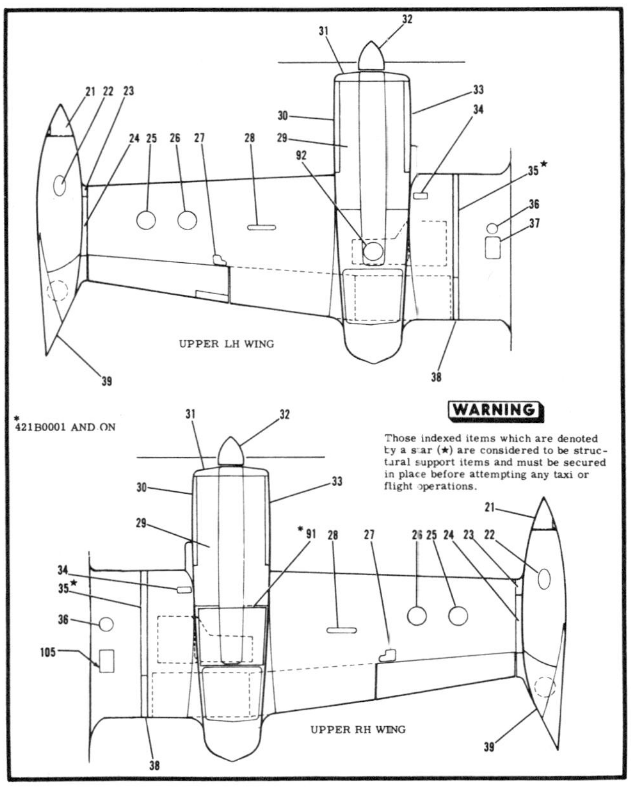

For locating inspection plates, refer to the service manual or ask an experienced mechanic.

Determining which plates and fairings to remove is often a problem when inspecting an aircraft type for the first time. The service manual should be consulted, but the best source of information will be to ask a veteran mechanic who is experienced on that type of aircraft. The cowlings should be placed in an appropriate storage rack.

8. Removal of interior, seats, carpets, and upholstery

Many aircraft have a requirement to inspect the structure and components of the systems that are located beneath the floor and in the sidewalls of the cabin. This will require the removal of many interior parts of the aircraft. Care should be taken to keep from damaging these parts. The seats and upholstery should also be properly stored to keep them from being soiled or damaged. The attachment method of the carpets should be carefully noted. Any placards or controls that are removed should be placed in a secure place to keep from being misplaced.

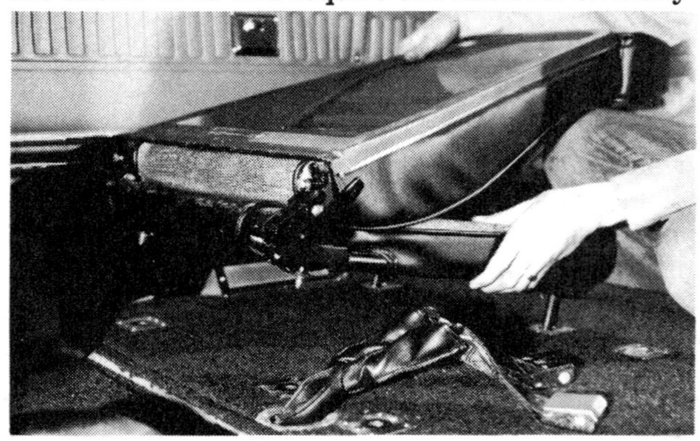

Before inspection interior parts must be removed.

AD notes on aircraft components should be checked for compliance with regulations.

9. General Aviation Airworthiness Alerts — AC No. 43-16

There is a publication available from the FAA called General Aviation Airworthiness Alerts — AC No. 43-16. This publication contains a list of problem areas that should be carefully inspected on each make and model of aircraft. When preparing to perform an inspection on an aircraft, the inspector should look up the make and model of the aircraft in the Alerts and write down on the checklist the items that apply to that aircraft.

The information found in the Alerts is acquired from all of the Malfunction and Defect Reports that are sent to the FAA by technicians in the field, performing maintenance on aircraft. All maintenance technicians are urged to participate in this program as it will aid them in obtaining information on problems to look for while inspecting an aircraft.

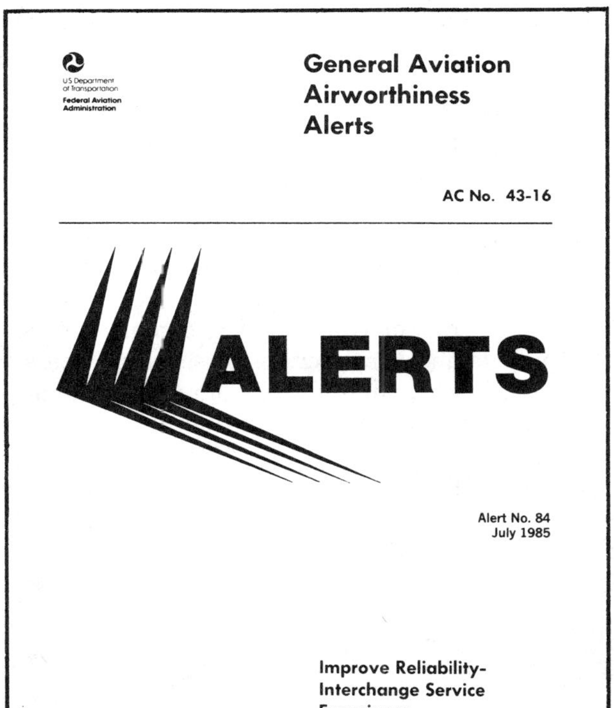

General Aviation airworthiness "Alerts" from the FAA contain information on problem areas.

B. Inspection Requirements

The items to be inspected on the airframe will differ between the various types of aircraft. A person inspecting an airframe must use a *checklist* to ensure that he does not overlook any inspection items. This checklist may be one designed and supplied by the manufacturer or one designed by someone else. This checklist must include the scope and detail listed in Appendix D of FAR 43.

1. Airframe inspection

The inspection of the airframe should be done in a logical and systematical manner. A recommended pattern to follow would be to begin the inspection in the interior of the aircraft, then moving to one of the wings, returning to the exterior of the fuselage, moving back to the empennage, then moving forward on the fuselage to the other wing and ending the airframe inspection on the front part of the fuselage and landing gear. Each inspector will have to develop his own pattern with different types of aircraft.

a. Interior inspection

The inspection of the interior of the aircraft requires that all seats, carpets, upholstery, and inspection panels, requiring removal, have been removed during the pre-inspection phase. A good flashlight and inspection mirror will be necessary to properly inspect many hidden items. *The items to be inspected may be completed in any sequence that is desired as long as none are overlooked.*

A typical inspection procedure of an interior of an aircraft is given as follows:

1. Check the operation and fit of all cabin doors, windows, stops, latches, locks, hinges, and attaching parts.

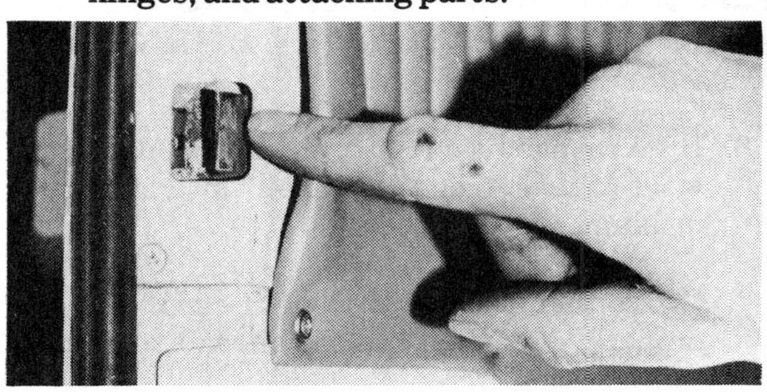

During an interior inspection, no item should be overlooked including door latches and locks.

2. Check the condition of door and window seals.

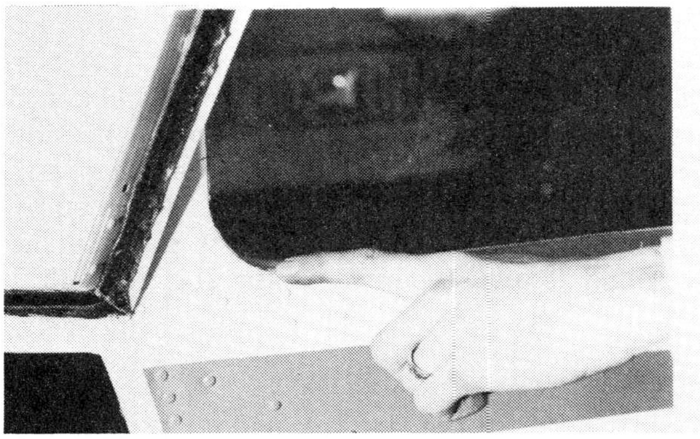

Attention to detail is important especially around windows and door seals.

3. Inspect the condition of the plexiglas windows and windshield.

4. Check the seats, upholstery, seat operation mechanism, seat tracks, and stops for proper operation and condition.

5. Check seat belts for condition, cleanliness, conformity to TSOC22, security of attachment, and locking of latches.

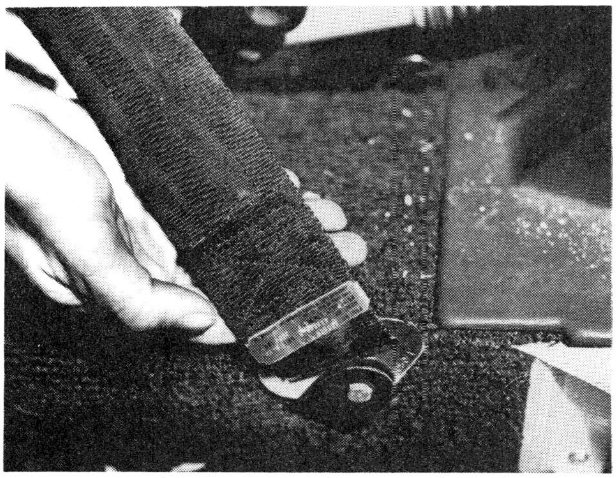

Among other things, seat belts should be checked for security of attachment.

6. Inspect condition of upholstery, carpets, visors, ash trays, and all interior furnishings.

7. Check that the airworthiness certificate is properly displayed and the aircraft registration is in the aircraft.

8. Perform a conformity check of installed equipment by observing if any unusual or different equipment for that type of aircraft is installed.

9. Check the operation and condition of fresh air vents, heat and defrost ducts and valves.

10. Inspect the baggage compartment for loose equipment, condition, door operation and locking.

Baggage compartments undergo abuse, so take a close look for possible damage.

11. Inspect the ELT for proper installation, battery replacement date, antenna connection condition, routing, and operation.

12. Inspect rudder pedals and attaching parts for operation, condition, and security of attachment.

13. Inspect brake master cylinders for operation, fluid level, attachment, and plumbing.

14. Check control yokes, slides, chains, cables, pulleys and turnbuckles for security, operation, safety, chafing, freedom of movement, rotation, and general condition.

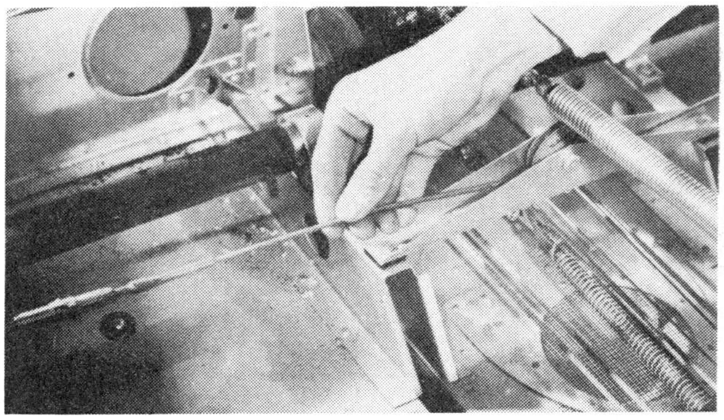

Control cables must be closely examined. Often a defect is not easily seen.

15. Inspect operation of the trim operating mechanisms, linkages, indicators, cables, and pulleys.

A close look under the instrument panel is necessary to spot hidden problems which could be disasterous.

16. Check the manually operated flap system for operation, locking, binding, security of attachment, and indicators for proper operation.

17. Check fuel selector and shut off valves for leaks, binding, detent feel, placarding, and operation.

18. Inspect fuel system plumbing for chafing, damage, leaks, security, and routing.

19. Check primer for leakage, operation, sticking, and locking.

20. Inspect the magnetic standby compass for leakage, fluid level, condition, mounting, and calibration on the compass card.

Magnetic compasses should not only be checked for operation, but to make sure the correction card is accurate.

21. Inspect all plumbing and electrical wiring behind instrument panel for routing, chafing, security of attachment, and leakage.

22. Inspect vacuum system filters and screens for cleanliness, security, and attachment of hose and lines.

23. Check all instruments for proper mounting, condition (if practical), for proper operation, operating limit marking, and attachment of wires and hoses.

24. Check instrument panel shock mounts for condition and movement of the panel.

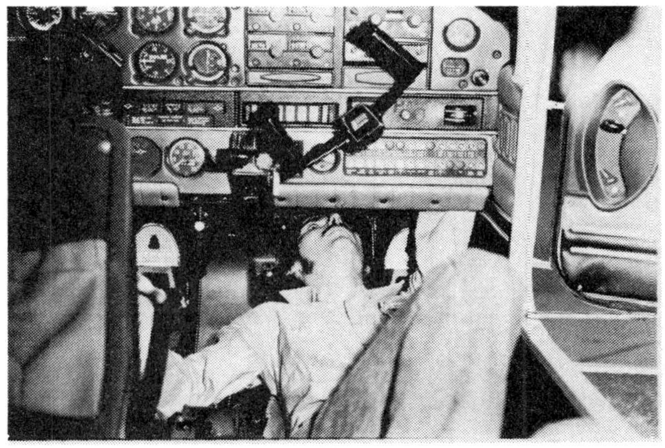

Inspecting behind the panel can be complicated, but it is an important part of the inspection.

25. Check engine controls for freedom, travel, operation, and condition.

26. Check for required placarding and marking of controls, switches, and instruments.

27. Check the operation of all miscellaneous knobs, and controls mounted in the cockpit.

28. Check all instrument and cabin lights for operation and condition.

29. Inspect all fuses, circuit breakers, switches, and wiring for operation, attachment, marking, and condition.

30. Inspect the battery and box, vents, solenoids, cables, and wiring for improper installation, operation, and general condition.

31. Check the battery for water level and proper state of charge.

32. Inspect the interior of the tail cone for general condition, corrosion, cracking, cable routing, pulley operation, and loose objects.

b. Wing inspection

1. Inspect external wing skin or fabric for general condition, deterioration, damage, and corrosion.
2. Inspect the internal structure for corrosion, damage, and general condition.
3. Inspect wing attachments for security.
4. Inspect external struts for condition and attachment.
5. Check pitot tube for attachment, heat, and plumbing.
6. Check stall warning switches or reeds for proper operation.
7. Check navigation and landing lights for operation, and security of mounting.
8. Inspect aileron for attachment, operation, and condition.
9. Check flaps for operation, condition, and security of attachment.

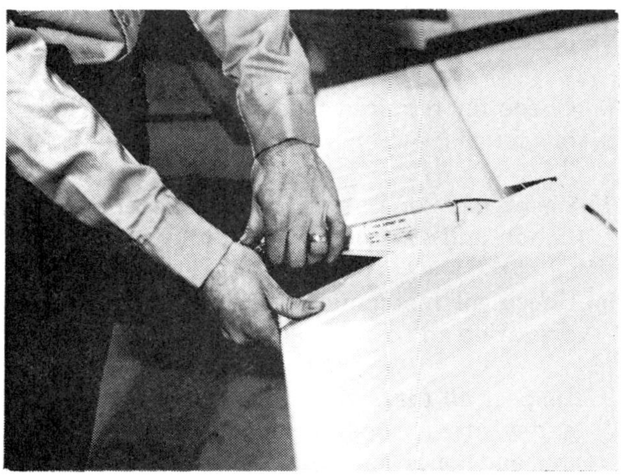

Control surface movement is critical because often these surfaces are "balanced".

10. Check aileron control system cables, pulleys, fairleads, push-pull rods, bearings, bellcranks, turnbuckles, and stops for proper operation, condition, and safety of attachment.
11. Check flap operating mechanisms for operation, lubrication, security of attachment, and freedom of movement.

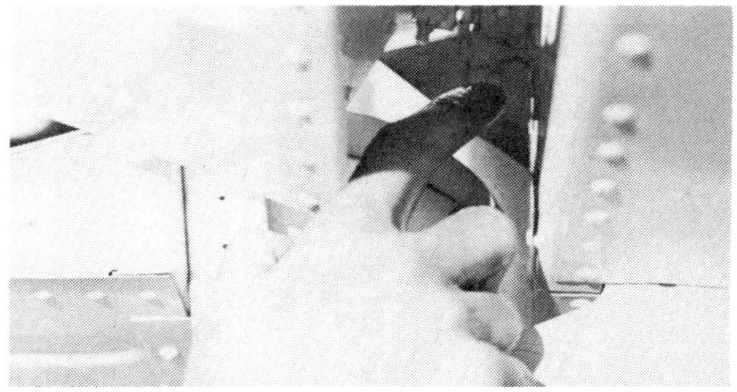

All control surface hinge points should be checked for condition and proper lubrication.

12. Inspect trim tab and system for proper operation, attachment, and general condition.
13. Inspect fuel tanks, fuel caps, vents, plumbing, and quantity indicating systems for leakage, proper operation, and marking of fuel filler opening.
14. Check fuel sumps and screens for cleaniness, and contamination.
15. Check condition of bonding straps and static wicks.

c. Fuselage inspection

1. Inspect the fabric or skin for condition, deterioration, corrosion, and damage.
2. Check the static ports for cleanliness and freedom from obstruction.
3. Inspect radio antenna for proper attachment, mounting, and condition.
4. Inspect internal parts through appropriate inspection panels for condition, attachment, and operation as applicable.
5. Inspect the cabin entrance step and operating mechanism for condition and proper operation.

d. Empennage inspection

1. Inspect the horizontal stabilizer for condition and security of attachment.

2. Inspect the elevator and hinges for condition, freedom of movement, travel, and security of attachment.

3. Inspect the elevator trim tab for condition, security of attachment and operation.

4. Inspect the vertical stabilizer for condition and security of attachment.

Control surface travel should be checked especially if it has been removed and re-installed.

5. Inspect the rudders for condition, freedom of movement, travel and security of attachment.

6. Inspect anti-collision beacons for condition and security.

7. Inspect navigation antenna for proper attachment and condition.

e. Landing gear inspection

1. Raise the aircraft so the gear is clear of the floor by jacking or hoisting.

A retraction test should be performed to check the entire mechanism.

2. Remove the wheels, inspect and repack the bearings, inspect wheels and tires, inflate tires to proper pressure.

3. Inspect brake linings, discs, clips, and wheel cylinders for wear, leakage, and condition.

4. Inspect axle and install wheel and brakes on axle and safety.

5. Deflate shock struts and check fluid level, inflate struts to recommended pressure.

6. Inspect rudder shock cords for condition, age, and necking.

7. Inspect tail wheel assembly and springs for condition, security of attachment, and operation of steering mechanism.

8. Inspect shimmy damper for security of attachment, leakage, fluid level, and for excessive wear in the attachment.

9. Inspect nose steering mechanism for wear, security of attachment, freedom of operation, condition, excessive wear, and centering mechanism for operation.

10. Check torque links or scissors for condition, wear, cracks, excessive play, and condition.

11. Inspect landing gear struts for security of attachment, leakage, cleanliness, and general condition.

12. Check landing gear retraction and extension mechanism for leakage, wear, damage, security of attachment, cleanliness, and general condition.

13. Check brake and hydraulic hoses and lines for leakage, chafing, proper support, damage, age hardening, and general condition.

Wheels, brakes, and tires should be checked for excessive wear and damage.

14. Check electrical switches and wiring for cleanliness, chafing, proper support, and general condition.

15. Inspect landing gear doors, linkages, hinges and operating mechanism for wear, damage, cleanliness, fit, and security of attachment, and general condition.

16. Retractable landing gear operational check procedures:

    a. Jack the aircraft clear of the floor.

    b. Check the retraction safety switch for proper operation and adjustment using the procedures specified in the service manual.

    c. Disconnect appropriate doors and linkages and secure out of the way of the gear operation.

    d. Operate retraction system until the downlocking mechanism is released. Check gear struts, linkages, cylinders, and rods for excessive clearances and wear.

    e. After checking for wear and clearances continue to retract the gear and observe the gear for proper operation, binding, chafing, operation of the uplocks and electrical switches.

    f. While the gear is in the retracted position check the uplock tension and clearances, operation of the landing gear up indicating lights, adjustment and operation of the throttle warning switches, lights, and horn.

    g. Extend the landing gear observing extension mechanism and gear linkages for proper operation, binding, chafing, and movement.

    h. Check the downlock for proper operation, tension, and clearance, indicating lights and switches for adjustment and operation.

    i. Check the downlock indicating lights and switches for adjustment and operation.

    j. Reconnect all the doors and linkages and safety.

    k. Retract the landing gear. Observe the operation of the doors and linkages. Check doors for fit, clearances, and tension.

    l. Extend the landing gear using the emergency extension mechanism and check for operation, downlock engagement and indicating lights for proper indication.

    m. Retract and extend the landing gear by the normal system to ensure proper operation.

    n. Remove the aircraft from the jacks and adjust the strut inflation as necessary for proper strut extension.

2. Engine inspection

The inspection of the engine should be as extensive as necessary to ensure that the engine is in an airworthy condition. The engine should be cleaned and its hoses, lines, and electrical wiring should be neatly clamped and supported from chafing and to avoid heat damage from the exhaust system.

The inspection of the engine may require some disassembly to perform a large number of the inspection items. A planned sequence should be used in addition to the checklist to make sure that no inspection details are omitted.

a. Internal engine condition

A differential compression test is used to determine cylinder condition.

The internal condition of the engine is determined by checking the compression of the cylinders and inspecting the oil screen to see if there are any metal particles adhering to it that have been strained out of the oil. The procedures for checking the cylinder compression and oil screen are as follows:

/1/ Cylinder compression

The differential pressure compression tester is the most satisfactory method of checking the cylinders to see that the valves and rings are not leaking excessively. Usually the top spark plugs and the leads on the bottom plugs are removed to prevent accidental firing of the cylinders when the propeller is rotated.

The spark plug adaptor for the tester is then inserted into the number 1 spark plug hole and tightened. A source of air is then connected to the tester. This air source should have a capacity in excess of 80 psi. The air pressure flowing through the orifice in the tester should be adjusted to the pressure as specified in the service manual, usually either 20 psi or 80 psi for the engine being tested.

The next step is to set the cylinder on either bottom center or top center of the compression stroke as specified by the manufacturer. Follow the manufacturer's procedures, open the air valve to determine the compression in the cylinder. Record the compression value of each cylinder on the check list. Using the firing order of the engine, check all cylinders in proper sequence. Caution should be taken to protect against the rapid movement of the propeller when the pressure tester air valve is opened.

All the cylinders should be approximately equal to each other in compression and each cylinder should be above 75% of the applied air pressure. If excessive leakage is noted, attempt to determine the cause of the leakage. This can be done by listening to determine if the air is escaping out of the exhaust pipe, carburetor, or engine breather. This will help determine what maintenance will be required to repair the excessive cylinder leakage.

/2/ Oil screen check

The removal of the oil screen or oil filter is required to determine if the engine is having excessive and destructive wear or deterioration. This is determined by checking to see if any metal particles are present on the screen and in the screen housing. Oil filters that are becoming popular on today's engines must be cut open and inspected. If metal particles are found, the source of the metal will have to be determined and a decision must be made as to whether the engine is airworthy or not.

b. Ignition system checks

The spark plugs should be removed. And, as each plug is removed, the *electrode end* should be examined for possible combustion deposits. This will often display the internal condition of the cylinder, operation of the fuel system, and the way the pilot is operating his engine. The plugs should then be cleaned, pressure tested, and gapped. Upon installation, new spark plug gaskets should be used and the plug torqued to the proper value.

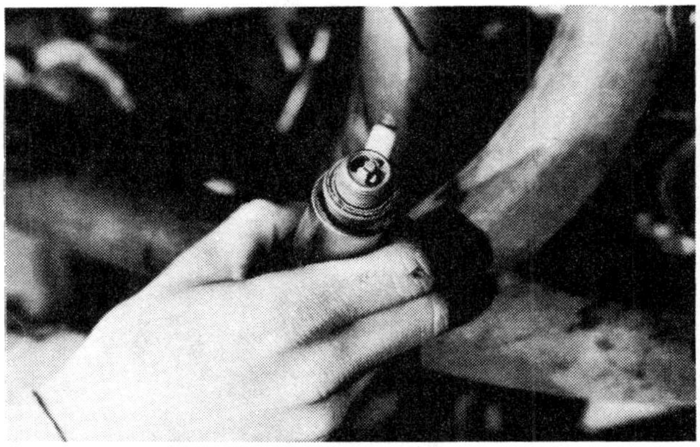

Each spark plug should be examined for deposits as it is removed.

Ignition leads should be checked for general condition, proper routing, cleanliness, condition of the plug ends, security, chafing, and heat damage.

The magnetos should be inspected in accordance with the particular manufacturer's recommendations of timing, breaker point condition, lubrication, security of mounting, internal oil leakage, lead attachment, and general condition. The magneto model and part number should be carefully checked against the airworthiness directives and service bulletins to see if any directives or bulletins apply to them. The propeller should be rotated to ensure that the impulse couplings (if installed) are functioning properly.

c. Exhaust system inspection

The exhaust system should be checked for leakage, security of mounting, cracks, warpage, and general condition. The heat shroud around the mufflers should be removed and the muffler carefully checked for leakage, discoloration, cracks and general condition. A flashlight and a mirror should be used to check the inside of the muffler for loose or missing flame tubes and baffles. The muffler should be checked against the airworthiness directives to see if any directives apply to it. The flexible air ducts or hoses should be checked for condition and security. If a turbosupercharger is installed it should be inspected in accordance with the manufacturer's recommendations.

d. Engine controls

The throttle, carburetor heat, mixture, cowl flap, oil cooler, propeller and heat controls should be checked for routing, chafing, security, safety, excessive wear, damage, and general condition. Each control should be operational checked for full travel, freedom, binding and proper operation. The throttle and mixture linkages should be checked for excessive wear and proper safety. The carburetor heat box and valve should be checked for wear and damage.

A general engine inspection includes checking for general condition and adjustment of accessories.

e. General engine inspection

The engine compartment should be checked for evidence of fuel, oil, and hydraulic leaks and the source of the leaks determined. All fuel, oil, and hydraulic hoses should be checked for condition, age, hardening, chafing, security, routing, and general condition. The cooling baffles and seals should be checked for cracks, security, mounting, and general condition. Studs and nuts should be checked for obvious defects and evidence of looseness. The intake system should be checked for security of attachment and for signs of leakage. The carburetor and fuel pump should be checked for security of attachment, safety, general condition, and leakage. The cylinders should be checked for broken fins, evidence of leakage, and general condition.

The oil cooler should be inspected for leakage, security of attachment, and general condition. The engine mount and vibration dampeners and mounts should be checked for cracks, corrosion, damage, security of attachment, deterioration, and general condition. All accessories should be checked for security of mounting, general condition and obvious defects. The dust cover should be removed from the starters and DC generators and the condition of the brushes and commutator checked. All electrical wiring and bundles should be checked for proper security, routing, and general condition. Inspect the firewall for leakage, damage, and general condition, check crankcase for cracks, leakage, and general condition. Inspect the breather tube and lines for obstruction, routing, security, and general condition. Alternator and generator drive belts should be checked for tension, deterioration, and general condition. The cowling should be inspected for cracks, condition of fasteners, damage, and general condition.

The smallest item, if overlooked during inspection, can cause the biggest problems.

3. Propeller inspection

The inspection of the propeller will require that the propeller spinner be removed so that the hub and mounting bolts can be inspected. The hub should be checked for cracks, leakage of grease and oil, corrosion, and general condition. The propeller mounting bolts should be checked for proper torque and safety. The pitch changing arms

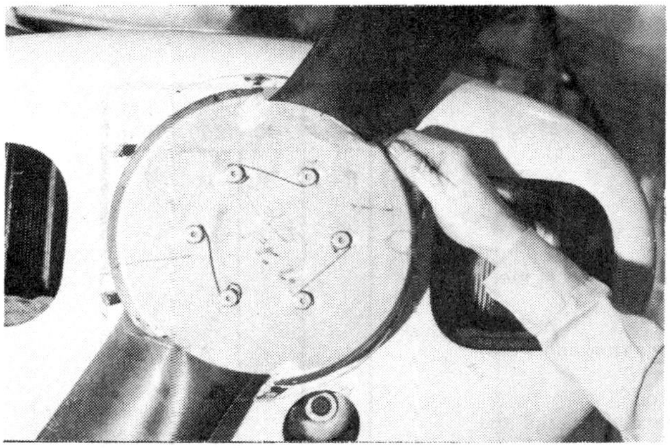

The propeller hub and assembly must be checked and properly safetied.

and bolts should be checked for condition and proper safety. The blades should be checked for nicks, scratches, corrosion, cracks, and obvious damage. The spinner and backplate should be

Propeller nicks and scratches must be properly removed to avoid in-flight blade failure.

checked for cracks and security of attachment. On a controllable propeller, the blades should be checked for proper movement in the hubs. The propeller hub and blade models should be checked for any airworthiness directives that may apply to them. The condition of the paint on the back and the tips of the blade should be checked.

4. Electronic installations

The inspection of the radios and electronic installations can be conducted during the inspection of the areas in which they are located, or inspected as an independent group depending upon the operating procedure of each individual shop.

The electronic equipment that is installed should be checked against the equipment list and weight and balance data to ensure that it has been properly recorded in the maintenance records. The equipment should be checked for security of attachment, improper installation procedures, bonding, condition of shock mounts, and general condition. The wiring and coaxial cables should be checked for proper routing, security of attachment, chafing, and general condition. The bonding and shielding of all the wiring and equipment should be checked for improper installation and poor condition.

Check mounting, security, and attachment of all electronic installations.

The emergency locator transmitter (ELT) should be checked for improper installation, battery replacement date, condition of the antenna and wiring. The unit should also be operated to ensure proper operation of the G-switch and the ELT.

The antennas should be checked for proper installation, loose mounting, grounding, and general condition.

C. Service and Repair Phase

The necessary servicing and repair needed to return the aircraft to service as airworthy should be completed as a separate function from the actual inspection. Only those service functions that can be easily included with the inspection items may be performed during the inspection phase — and then only if they do not upset the inspection procedure.

The requirements of the service manual for each aircraft model should be followed to determine the items that are to be serviced, type of service required, method of application, time interval between each service interval, and products to be used to complete the servicing.

2-18 GROUND HANDLING, SERVICING AND INSPECTION — 421 SERVICE MANUAL

		50	100	200	Spl Insp
ENGINE GROUP					
	CAUTION Ground magneto primary circuit before working on the engine.				
1.	Engine - Wash, check for security of accessories		★		
2.	Cowling - Wash, check for cracks, evidence of abrasion and wear			★	
3.	Induction Air Filter - Clean				6
4.	Induction Manifold - Check connections for condition		★		
5.	Engine Oil Pressure System - Check for leaks, bends, cracks and security		★		
6.	Engine Oil Filter - Change oil filter element and inspect adapters.		★		
7.	Engine Oil - Change		★		
8.	Engine Oil Separator - Inspect and clean element. Refer to Service Chart				6
9.	Engine Compartment - Visually check for condition, oil leaks, fuel leaks, etc.		★		
10.	Engine Controls - Check travel and security		★		
11.	Engine Wire Bundle - Check for condition and security		★		
12.	Engine Mounts - Check for condition and security		★		
13.	Engine Compartment Hoses - Fuel, (check fuel lines under pressure) Oil Vacuum, etc. - Check deterioration, leaks, discoloration, bleaching and rubber hoses for stiffness	★			
14.	Cylinder Compression - Refer to Manufacturer's Service Bulletin M73-19		★		
15.	Engine Cylinders, Rocker Box Covers and Pushrod Housings - Check for fin damage, cracks, oil leakage, security of attachment and general condition		★		
16.	Crankcase, Oil Sump and Accessory Section - Inspect for cracks and evidence of oil leakage. Check bolts and nuts for looseness and retorque as necessary			★	
17.	Plugs - Clean and rotate (top right to bottom left, top left to bottom right)		★		
18.	Ignition Cables - Check condition and security		★		
19.	Magneto - Check timing, breaker gap and security				14
20.	Alternator - Check brushes, leads, bearings and slip rings				7
21.	Starter - Check brushes, commutator and electrical connections		★		
22.	Propeller Governor - Check for oil leaks, condition and security			★	
23.	Pumps - Fuel, Vacuum and Autopilot - Check for leaks, condition and security		★		
24.	Turbocharger - Check for condition, bulges, warps and security		★		
25.	Engine Exhaust System- Check for security, cracks, bellows and spring tension	★			
26.	Engine Exhaust System- Check for security, cracks, and spring tension- Visually inspect slip joint seals.	★			
27.	Waste Gate Valve, Variable Absolute Pressure Controller and Rate Controller - Check for condition and security. Visually check springs and linkage			★	
28.	Manifold Pressure Relief Valve - Visually check for obstructions, condition, security and proper operation			★	
29.	Engine Oil Screen - Check for removal. (Refer to expanded paragraph)	★			
30.	Engine Compartment Fire Extinguisher - Check system pressure, condition and security		★		

Figure 2-7. Inspection Chart (Sheet 3)

Copy of a page from a service manual showing equipment requirements.

The servicing required on the airframe consists of the lubrication of the control system moving parts, replacement or cleaning of the vacuum system filters, draining of the fuel sumps and gascolator, cleaning of the fuel screens and filters, testing the charge and condition of the battery, adding water to the battery, cleaning the battery and battery compartment, servicing of the battery sump, drain and vent system.

Battery servicing is important to control corrosion and ensure dependable starting power.

The servicing of the landing gear and brake system consists of adding fluid and air to the struts, lubrication of the landing gear, lubrication and cleaning of the wheel bearing, inflation of the tires, adding fluid to the brake and hydraulic reservoir, adding fluid to the shimmy damper, and the cleaning of gear switches and rollers.

Servicing of the engine and propeller consists of adding the correct type and amount of oil to the crankcase, cleaning or replacement of the carburetor air intake filter, cleaning or replacement of the oil filter or screens, cleaning and draining of the carburetor, fuel system sumps and screens, lubrication of the control linkages, lubrication of propeller, checking and adding nitrogen to the propeller accumulator, filing of minor nicks and scratches on the propeller blades, repainting of the propeller face and tips.

The repair phase consists of repairing the discrepancies that were discovered during the look phase of the inspection. This phase can also be used to comply with airworthiness directive and service bulletin requirements that are due or will become due prior to the next scheduled inspection of the aircraft.

D. Post Inspection

The post inspection phase consists of preparing the aircraft for its return to service. This phase should be accomplished with a great eye for small details as the owner of the aircraft will judge the quality of the inspection by the way his aircraft looks and runs after the inspection is completed.

1. Installation of interior and inspection panels

The installation of the interior, carpets, upholstery, and seats should be done with great care and attention to detail. The original fasteners should be used to attach the upholstery and contact cement or velcro tapes can be used to hold carpets in their proper place. The seat belts should be neatly arranged and the controls checked for freedom of movement.

Inspection panels and fairings should be installed in their proper position using new hardware to replace damaged or worn out screws and nuts. The screws should be installed secure enough to properly hold the panel but not so tight as to make removal nearly impossible. *Remember: you may be the one that has to remove them at the next inspection.*

2. Cleanliness of the aircraft

The cleanliness of the aircraft, both interior and exterior may be one of the few obvious signs to the aircraft owner that anything was accomplished on his aircraft for the several hundred dollars that the inspection has cost him. It is very important that the aircraft and engine be thoroughly cleaned and neat in appearance.

A clean exterior of an airplane helps to protect the surface against corrosion.

The engine compartment should be washed with a suitable cleaning solvent using an air pressure cleaning gun to remove all oil and dirt residue.

The interior should be vacuumed and cleaned, the instrument glass and panel dusted and cleaned. All the interior windows cleaned and ash trays emptied. All knobs and control switches cleaned. All of the miscellaneous articles located in the cabin and baggage compartment should be secured and neatly stowed away.

The airframe exterior should be washed and cleaned. The belly should be thoroughly cleaned of all oil and exhaust residue. The windows should be cleaned and protected with an approved *static free* wax. Exposed portions of the landing gear struts should be cleaned and wiped with an approved lubricant.

Cleaning the aircraft prior to returing it to service is important as often it is the only change an aircraft owner will detect after an inspection.

3. Functional checks

The functional checks required after an inspection has been completed will vary from one type of aircraft to another, but will consist of an operational check of almost every system installed in the aircraft to ensure they will perform properly.

The airframe systems to be checked consist of: landing and navigation lights, anti-collision lights or strobes, instrument lights, wing flap operation, flight control systems, radio and navigation equipment where practical, instrument operation where practical, fuel selector valve and system, stall warning system, heating and ventilating systems, and pitot heat operation.

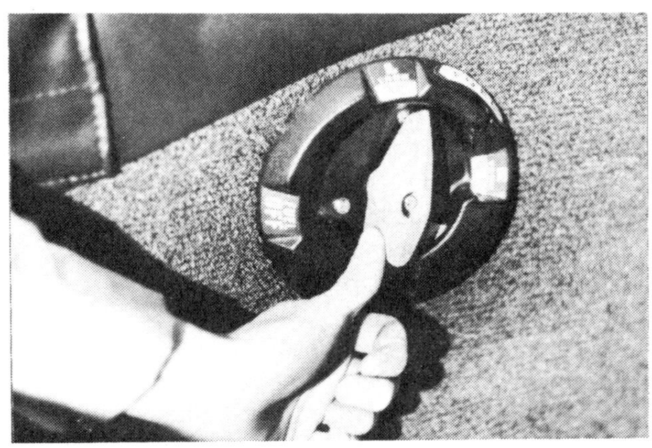

A functional check of each of the aircraft's systems helps to avoid in-flight problems.

The engine and propellers should operate properly, according to the manufacturer's recommendations. FAR Part 43.15 also requires that the engine be operated to determine satisfactory operation in accordance with the manufacturer's recommendation of power output, (both static and idle rpm), magnetos, fuel and oil pressure, and cylinder and oil temperature.

Functional checks may also include actual flight testing of the aircraft.

The functional checks on the engine consist of a fuel pressure check to ensure that none of the fuel system is leaking, engine runup to check the operation of the magnetos, propeller, carburetor heat, idle speed and idle mixture, maximum static rpm, fuel and oil pressures, cylinder and oil temperature, hydraulic system pressure, generator or alternator operations, instrument vacuum pressure, de-icing or anti-icing system operation. After engine shutdown a check should be made for evidence of fluid leakage in the engine compartment.

4. *Return to service procedures*

The return to service phase is the completion of the proper entries in the aircraft and maintenance records of all the work performed on the aircraft.

The requirements for the return to service entry for a 100-hour inspection are found in FAR Part 43.11 and consists of the following information: type of inspection, date of the inspection, aircraft time in service, certification statement, signature, and the certificate number. An entry commonly in use is as follows:

Sample Entry

May 30, 1986 *Total Time 488 hours*

I certify that this aircraft (or engine) has been inspected in accordance with a 100-hour inspection and was determined to be in airworthy condition.

Russ Fellows

A&P No. 1607438

The common practice is to make an entry in the airframe record and *another* entry in the engine and propeller record for the return to service after the inspection has been completed.

When repair work or airworthiness directives have been accomplished, it is common practice to include these items in a paragraph between the date and time in service and the inspection certification part of the entry. An entry commonly in use is as follows:

Combination Sample Entry

May 30, 1986 *Total Time 488 hours*

Battery replaced, left main gear tire replaced, new brake lining installed on both main gear, AD 76-03-99, revision date, August 14, 1977, complied with by replacing the fuel selector in accordance with Paragraph B, Service bulletin SE 78-10 complied with.

I certify that this aircraft has been inspected in accordance with a 100-hour inspection and was determined to be in airworthy condition.

Greg Coombs

A&P No. 1607438

QUESTIONS:

1. Must an airworthiness directive that is due be complied with before a 100-hour inspection can be approved for return to service?

2. Must service bulletins on most small aircraft be complied with before the aircraft can be approved for return to service?

3. List the things you would inspect on the seat belts installed in an aircraft.

4. What two certificates must be in the aircraft at all times?

5. List the inspection requirements of the ELT.

6. List the inspection requirements for the aircraft battery.

7. List the inspection requirements for an operational check of the retractable landing gear.

8. What are two checks that are accomplished to determine the internal condition of the engine?

9. List the inspection requirements on a magneto during a 100-hour inspection?

SECTION V

Maintenance Records

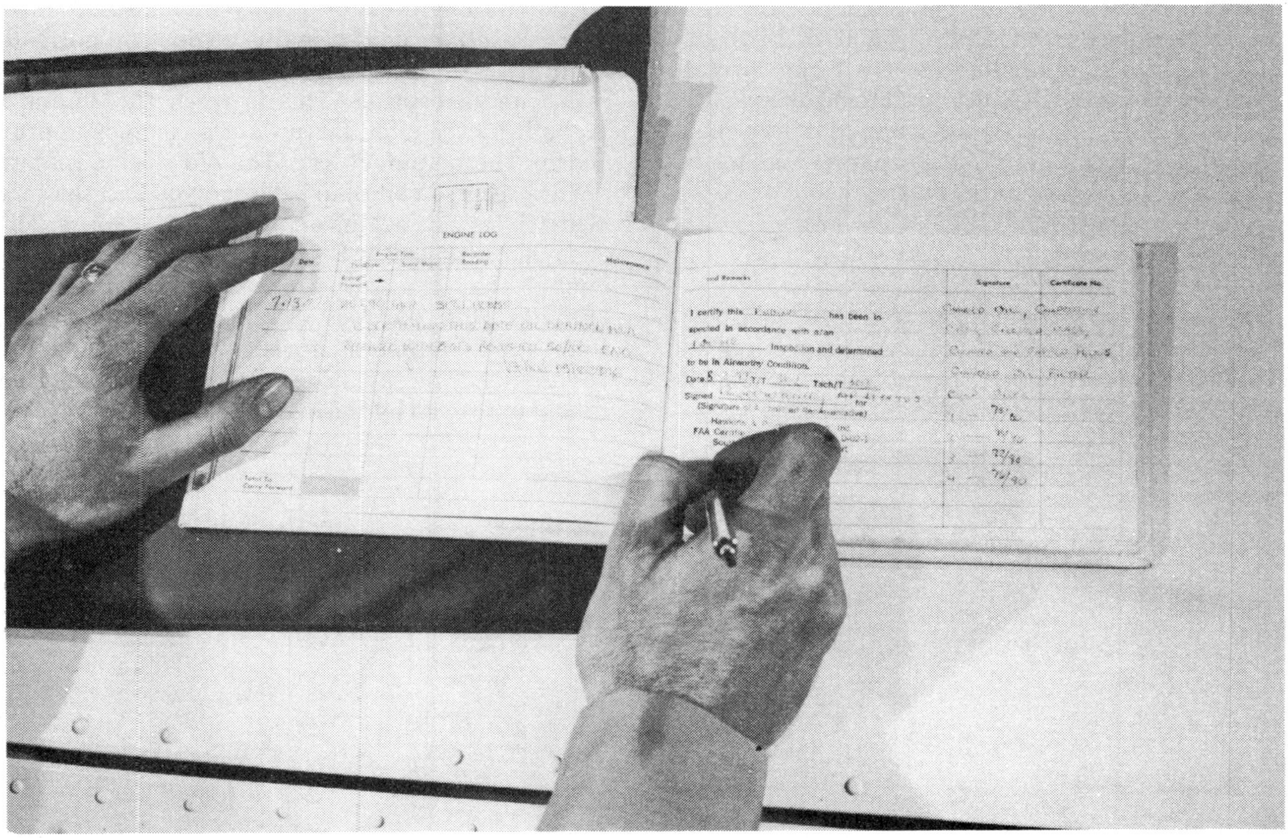

The requirement for maintaining appropriate records are contained in FAR Part 91.173. It is important that a licensed mechanic make the correct logbook entries after an inspection.

A. *Owners Responsibilities*

The owner or operator is primarily responsible for having and maintaining the maintenance records for his aircraft. He is required to present them to the maintenance personnel and ensure that maintenance personnel make appropriate entries in the aircraft and maintenance records indicating the aircraft has been released to service. Upon the transfer or sale of the aircraft he is required to transfer the appropriate records to the new owner. The owner or operator is required to present his records for inspection to the FAA and the National Transportation Safety Board when requested to do so.

B. *Records Required*

The requirements for the appropriate maintenance records are contained in FAR 91.173. This regulation requires that the owner or operator of an aircraft keep and maintain a record of the alterations, maintenance, 100-hour, annual, progressive and other inspections required on his aircraft, on each engine, propeller, rotor, and appliance on his aircraft. The owner must also maintain a record of the total time in service, current status of life-limited parts, time since overhaul on all items requiring overhaul on a specific time basis, current status of applicable airworthiness directives, AD revision date, the method of compliance, and if it's a recurring AD, the time action is due, and a current list of major alterations that apply to his aircraft.

1. Airframe record

The airframe record is commonly called the *aircraft log*book on the majority of general aviation aircraft. This logbook is used to record the time in service, maintenance, alterations, inspections and AD compliance on the airframe and its associated components and appliances. On large aircraft, turbine powered aircraft, and helicopters, this logbook may contain only a record of the maintenance of the airframe with separate logs for the appliances, component parts, and rotors.

2. Engine records

The engine log is maintained to record the time in service, maintenance, alterations, inspection, and AD compliance on the engine, propeller and its associated parts and appliances on most of the general aviation aircraft. Large and turbine powered aircraft and helicopters often use separate logs for the propeller, appliances and parts of the engine that are changed frequently or have life-limited components.

a. Rebuilt engine records

When an engine is originally manufactured, the *time-in-service* on the engine begins and normally continues until the engine is retired from service with one exception. This is when the engine is rebuilt by the manufacturer or an agency approved by the manufacturer. The old engine maintenance records can than be destroyed and the total time in service begins again from *zero hours*. This rule is contained in FAR 91.175 and it should be noted that the key word in the regulation is *rebuilt*. This rule *does not* apply to those engines that are remanufactured, reconditioned, or overhauled by aviation companies other than those approved by the manufacturer.

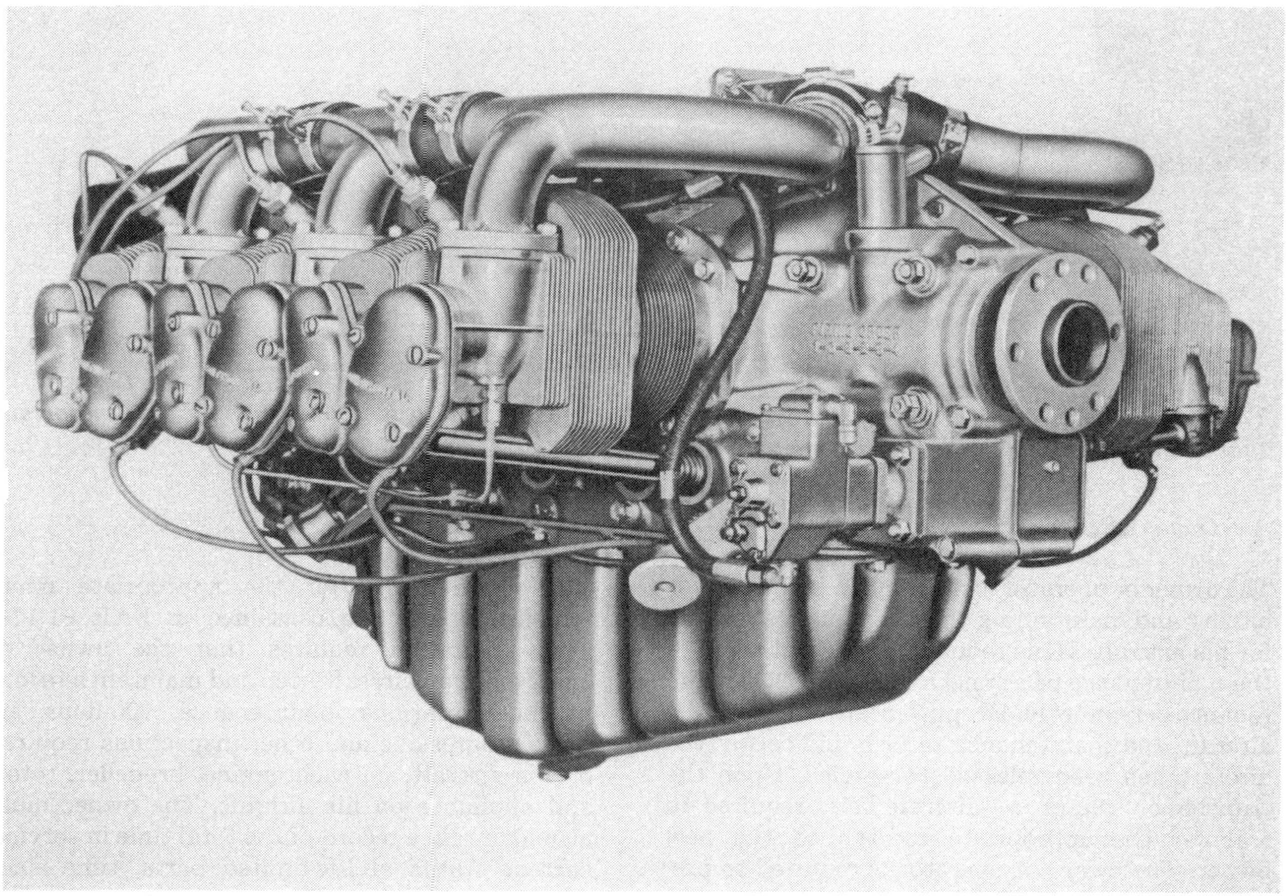

When an engine is rebuilt by the manufacturer, or its approved agency, its time-in service records begin with 0 hours.

3. Propeller records

The propeller maintenance record is required to maintain the total time in service, maintenance, alterations, inspections and AD compliance on a propeller. On most light general aviation aircraft, this record is combined with the engine log as the propeller usually stays with the same engine throughout its time in service. As the trend towards exchanging engines and propellers continues, it may soon be necessary to use a separate maintenance record to comply with the requirements of FAR 91.173 in properly documenting the time in service and maintenance on a propeller.

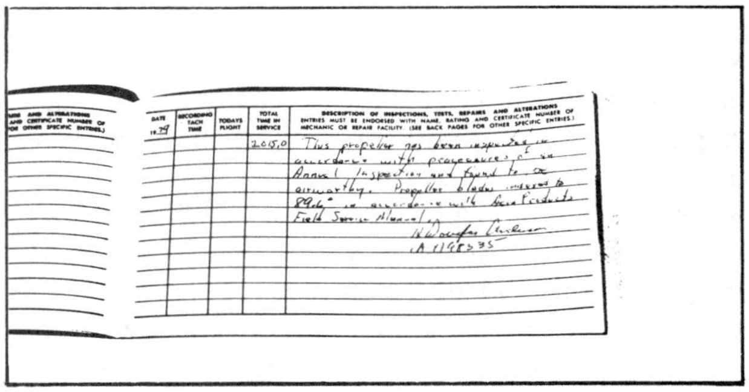

Propeller records should be kept in a separate logbook because an engine will often be separated from the propeller during an overhaul.

Helicopter rotors have special records to help determine the time-in-service status.

4. Rotor records

A special record is required on the rotors of a helicopter or rotorcraft to maintain the time in service, maintenance, alterations, and AD compliance. The rotors on a helicopter are usually a life-limited part and the time in service on the rotors can easily be determined if a separate record, other than the airframe log, is used to document the time-in-service. If the airframe log is used to document the maintenance and time-in-service, the log must contain sufficient information to clearly establish the status of the time-in-service of the rotors.

5. Appliance records

Whenever an appliance is installed on an airframe or engine and it is considered a life-limited or a required-time-overhaul-component, it must have a record of its time in service, maintenance, alterations and AD compliance. A separate record of the appliance would be the most appropriate method of documenting this information. If the airframe or engine log is used to document this information, it must contain sufficient information to clearly establish the status of the time in service of these appliances.

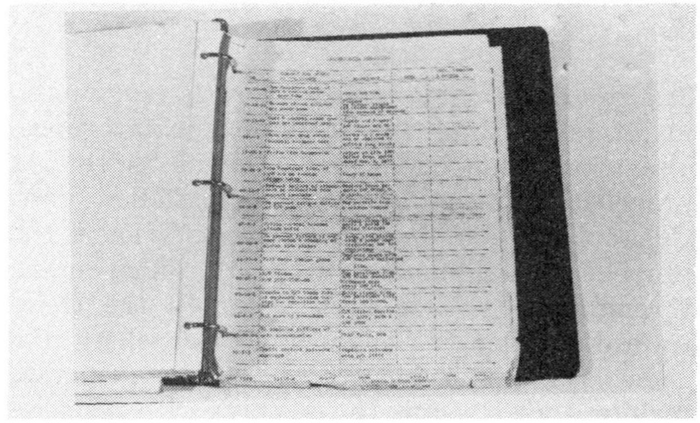

Separate logbooks for applicance is usually recommended for fast and accurate reference.

Each time an applicance is installed, an appropriate logbook entry is required to determine time-in-service.

6. Airworthy parts tag

Certificated repair stations frequently use special parts condition *tags* to document the condition of parts and appliances. This tag is also used as a maintenance record and the time-in-service and overhaul times can be recorded on them. When a part or appliance is repaired or overhauled, this tag is also considered the maintenance release or the return to service authorization for the individual appliance or parts and should be retained in the logs for further reference.

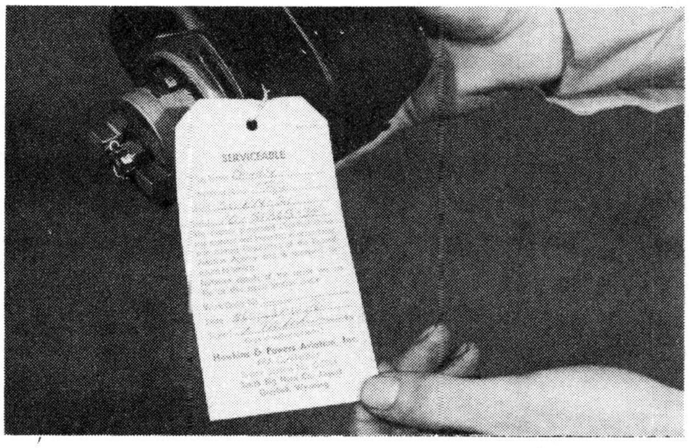

Airworthiness parts tags, used by certified repair station, document condition of parts.

7. Airworthiness directive record

The record of airworthiness directive compliance is usually incorporated into the body of the maintenance record entries. A separate record can also be used for this purpose or a combination of recording them in a body of the maintenance record entries. Often a separate record would make it easier to research and determine AD requirements.

Appendix A of this book has a suggested format that would satisfy the requirements of FAR 91.173 and provide the owner and maintenance personnel with an easy and reliable method of documenting and researching the AD compliance on an aircraft.

C. Format of Maintenance Records

There is no specified format or form for maintenance records. The records can be combined or separate in nature. Whatever is the most advantageous, works and satisfies the requirement of FAR 91.173 is acceptable. The important thing is to have a system that will provide the necessary information. It does not have to be a bound record such as the traditional logbooks. But, if separate unbound pages are used, it may be desirable to number the pages in the book.

Separate records for each engine, propeller and appliance may be desirable when life-limited parts are affected or if a large fleet operator desires to change components from one aircraft to another.

1. Required record information

The maintenance records should be identified as to the aircraft registration number, make, model, serial number, and location.

Information to be included in the records consists of: the total time in service of the items, the current status of life-limited parts, the time since last overhaul of items requiring overhaul on a time basis, current status of applicable airworthiness directives including the method of compliance, revision date, and if a recurring AD, the time or date when the next action is required, and a list of current major alterations to each airframe, engine, propeller, and appliance.

When maintenance is performed, the date of the completion of the work, a description or reference to data acceptable to the FAA of the work performed and the name, signature, and the certificate number of the person approving the work for return to service must be included in the maintenance record.

D. Retention of Maintenance Records

FAR Part 91.173 allows the owner to discard certain parts of the records after they have served their purpose. It also lists the records that must be retained. Records that must be retained are called *permanent records* and records that may be discarded are called *temporary records.*

1. Permanent records

Permanent records are those that contain the total time in service of the airframe, the current status of life-limited parts, the time since last overhaul of items to be overhauled on a time basis, the current status of the inspections required on the aircraft and its appliances, the current status of applicable airworthiness directives and the method of compliance, revision date, and if the AD is recurring, the time and date when the next action is required, and a current list of the major alterations to each airframe, engine, propeller, rotor, and appliance. These records must be retained and transferred to the new owner if the aircraft is sold.

2. Temporary records

The maintenance record entries for maintenance and inspection, excluding those that fall in the category of permanent records, shall be retained until the work is repeated or superceded by other work or for one year after the work is performed. This does not mean that these records must be discarded, but allows the owner to discard them if he so desires.

E. Lost or Destroyed Records

Whenever the maintenance records are lost or destroyed, the owner is responsible for starting a new record. One acceptable method of starting a new record would be for the owner or operator to make a notarized statement in the new record describing the loss and establishing the time in service. Establishing the time in service can be done by a research of other records that may have that information.

The current status of the inspection on the aircraft, the status of life-limited parts, times since last overhaul, and a current list of major alterations will also have to be determined. One concept that is being used is that if the status of these items is unknown, they are considered to be due at that time. This could prove to be very expensive for the owner of the aircraft. The status of applicable airworthiness directives would have to be determined. This requires a detailed inspection to determine compliance with all applicable airworthiness directives.

F. Recording of Major Repairs and Alterations

Whenever a major repair or major alteration is performed on an aircraft, it must be returned to service by the use of a FAA Form 337, *major repair and alteration* form. This form is initated by the mechanic performing the work and completed by the authorized person returning the completed work to service.

A certificated repair station may substitute his maintenance release or work order in place of the Form 337 for major repairs but he must use a Form 337 for major alterations.

QUESTIONS:

1. Who is primarily responsible for the maintenance records of an aircraft?
2. Must an owner of an aircraft present his maintenance records to the FAA if they request him to do so?
3. When can an engine that has been in service be returned to zero time in service?
4. Why is a separate record needed on a rotor of a helicopter?
5. When may it be necessary or more desirable to use a separate maintenance record for a propeller on an aircraft?
6. List the items that make up the permanent maintenance records on an aircraft?
7. What FAA form is used to approve a major alteration for return to service?
8. If the maintenance records are lost, who must initiate a new set of records?
9. How long must the information in the temporary maintenance records be retained?

SECTION VI

Maintenance Record Content and Entries

A. Aircraft Repair Entries

The minimum content of a maintenance record entry is listed in FAR 43.9 and consists of the completion date of the work performed, a description or reference to data acceptable to the FAA, the name and if returned to service, the signature and certificate number of the person approving the aircraft, airframe, engine, propeller, or appliance for return to service.

A typical sample entry is given as follows:

Sample Entry

June 6, 1985

Replaced the alternator on the left engine.

John Doe

A&P No. 1643872

1. Certificated repair station entries

Certificated repair stations are allowed to use an entry procedure that is different from maintenance personnel who return their work to service with the authorization of their mechanics certificate.

The procedure used by a certificated repair station for a major repair is to give the customer a *signed* work order upon which the maintenance is recorded. A duplicate copy of the work order is retained, and a maintenance release statement is placed in the owner's maintenance record, indicating the number of the work order, and signed by an authorized representative of the repair station. A sample maintenance release statement follows:

Sample Entry

The aircraft, airframe, aircraft engine, propeller, or appliance identified above was repaired and inspected in accordance with current regulations of the FAA and is approved for return to service.

Pertinent details of the repair are on file at this repair station under order:

No. 286 Date: June 6, 1985

Signed signature of authorized representative for

James Rogers

Repair Station Name Rogers Aircraft Ser

Certificate Number 564 - 14

Address Tyler, Oklahoma

B. Aircraft Inspection Entries

The maintenance record entries for the approval for return to service after inspections have been performed are specified in FAR Part 43.11. This regulation requires an entry in the maintenance records containing the date of the inspection, total time in service, certification statement, type of inspection, signature, and certificate number of the person approving or disapproving for return to service of the aircraft, airframe, engine, propeller, or appliance.

1. Annual inspection entry

An annual inspection can be signed off in the maintenance records as airworthy or unairworthy depending on the condition of the aircraft. A sample entry for the approval for the return to service after an annual inspection is as follows:

Sample Entry

June 6, 1985 Total Time 550 hours

I certify that this aircraft has been inspected in accordance with an annual inspection and was determined to be in airworthy condition.

George L. Smith

I.A. No. 1436721

a. Unairworthy inspection procedure

When an inspector completes an inspection and finds that the aircraft is unairworthy, he enters the completion of the inspection in the maintenance records indicating the aircraft's unairworthiness and a list of discrepancies are given to the owner of the aircraft. The owner is then required to have the discrepancies repaired before he can fly the aircraft.

These discrepancies are signed off by the appropriate person in the maintenance records as a repair entry, returning the aircraft to service. A sample entry indicating the completion of an annual inspection as unairworthy is as follows:

Sample Entry

June 6, 1985 Total Time 820 hours

I certify that this aircraft has been inspected in accordance with an annual inspection and a list of discrepancies and unairworthy items dated June 6, 1985 has been provided for the aircraft owner.

Thomas Kingery

I.A. No. 1643782

A letter to the aircraft's owner, listing the discrepancies that made the aircraft unairworthy, would be the best method of ensuring complete protection for the inspector and gives the proper notification to the owner.

Sample Letter

Asper, Iowa
June 6, 1985

Mr. James Johnson
126 Norwood Drive
Asper, Iowa

Dear Mr. Johnson,

This is to certify that on June 6, 1985, I completed an annual inspection on your aircraft Cessna 172L, Serial No. 17264837, N 2863A, located at the Northwoods Airports, and found it to be in unairworthy condition for the following reasons:

1. Left magneto has severely burned contact points.

2. Flame tubes in the muffler are broken loose.

Your aircraft will be considered to be in airworthy condition when the above listed discrepancies have been corrected and approved for return to service by a person authorized in Part 43 of the FAR.

John M. Smith

I.A. No. 1643782

2. 100-Hour inspection entry

A 100-hour inspection may be signed off in the maintenance records as airworthy or unairworthy, depending on the condition of the aircraft. This is accomplished by using the same procedures as listed in the preceding paragraphs and substituting "100-hour" in place of the "annual" wording.

A sample entry for the completion of a 100-hour inspection is as follows:

Sample Entry

June 6, 1985 Total Time 624 hours

I certify that this aircraft has been inspected in accordance with a 100-hour inspection and was determined to be in airworthy condition.

John Lawson

A&P No. 1642375

3. Progressive inspection entry

A sample entry for the approval for return to service after a progressive inspection is as follows:

Sample Entry

June 6, 1985 Total Time 624 hours

I certify that in accordance with a progressive inspection program, a routine inspection of the left wing and a detailed inspection of the engine were performed in accordance with a progressive inspection and the aircraft is approved for return to service.

Harold B. Nelson
A&P No. 1238645

4. Approved inspection program entry

An approved inspection program entry will include the kind of inspection conducted and a statement that the inspection was performed in accordance with the instructions and procedures for the inspection program selected by the owner or operator of the airplane.

If any defects or discrepancies discovered during the inspection are not repaired a signed and dated list of those discrepancies will be given to the aircraft owner or operator.

An entry for an approved inspection would be as follows:

Sample Entry

June 21, 1985 Total Time 1428 hours

I certify that in accordance with an Approved Inspection Program, a 50-hour inspection was performed in accordance with the Starjet approved inspection manual and the aircraft is approved for return to service.

Robert B. Johnson
A&P No. 1423876

C. Airworthiness Directive Compliance Entries

The information required in the maintenance records for the compliance of airworthiness directives is given in Part 91.173 of the FAR. The requirements consist of the recording of the date, total time, AD number, AD revision date, method of compliance and if the AD requires recurring action, the time and date when the next action is required, name, signature, and certificate number.

The recording of AD compliance can be maintained in the body of a logbook entry and/or kept as a separate listing in the maintenance records.

1. One-time AD compliance entry

Sample Entry

June 30, 1985 Total Time 826 hours

AD 76-03-05, revision date, Feb. 17, 1976, complied with by installing bracket in accordance with Paragraph B.

Fred Williams
A&P No. 1432652

2. Recurring AD compliance entry

Sample Entry

June 26, 1985 Total Time 1248 hours

AD 76-05-04, revision date, July 12, 1976, complied with by inspecting the stabilizer attachment in accordance with Paragraphs A and B. Next inspection due at 2248 hours.

John Lawson
A&P No. 1438673

3. AD compliance listing format and entries

A listing format may be used to show when the AD's were complied with and what method was used for the compliance. Some logbooks have provisions for these entrys. See page 51 for a sample listing format and how it is used.

D. Form 337, Major Alteration and Repair

In completing the form, the person performing the repair fills out the form except for the approval for return to service block. This block will be filled out when the repair is inspected by an authorized person. The back of the form is used to describe the repair and the approved data that was followed to perform the repair. It should be noted that approved information and instructions were followed in making the repair and these instructions must be identified and listed, the inspector can only approve the repair for return to service if approved data and instructions were used to perform the repair and the work was performed in an airworthy manner.

A Form 337 completed sample copy may be found in the following pages.

1. Disposition of Completed Form 337

Two copies of Form 337 must be completed and signed. The original copy should be provided to the aircraft owner to be placed in the aircraft maintenance records, and one copy should be sent to the local FAA General Aviation District Office within 48 hours of the approval for return to service of the aircraft, engine, propeller, or appliance that was repaired.

E. Preventive Maintenance Recording Requirements

The owner or operator of an aircraft is allowed to perform certain maintenance functions of a minor nature that requires performing no complex disassembly or reassembly. These are classed as preventive maintenance and are listed in Appendix A of the FAR Part 43.

When these maintenance functions are performed by the owner or operator there is *no* requirement that these items be entered in the maintenance records. If a certificated mechanic were to perform any of these same items on somebody elses aircraft he must enter the items in the maintenance records as a *minor repair.*

QUESTIONS:

1. List the five items that are to be included in an approval for return to service after a repair was completed.

2. Who can approve the aircraft for return to service after maintenance has been performed in a certificated repair station?

3. List the minimum information required to approve an aircraft for return to service following a 100-hour inspection.

4. When an annual inspection is completed and the aircraft is unairworthy the list of unairworthy items must be given to the owner and another copy must be sent to the local General Aviation District Office within how many hours?

5. Can a 100-hour inspection be signed off as unairworthy using the procedure that is used to declare an annual inspection unairworthy?

6. List the minimum required information used to sign off a recurring airworthiness directive.

7. How many copies of the FAA Form 337 are required to approve a major repair to service?

8. Who gets the copies of the FAA Form 337?

AIRWORTHINESS DIRECTIVE RECORD

AIRCRAFT MAKE: **MODEL:** **SERIAL NUMBER:** **N NUMBER:**

AD Number	Date of Revision	Subject	Date of Compliance	Total Time At Compliance	Method of Compliance	One Time	Recurring	Next Due Date/ Time	Name Signature Number
76-03-05	2-17-76	Bracket Installation	6-30-78	826 Hrs.	Install bracket i/a/w Para. b.	x			John Larson A&P 00110000
76-05-04	7-12-76	Stab. Attach. Inspection	6-26-78	1248 Hrs.	Inspected Stab. Attach i/a/w Para. a & b		x	2248 Hrs	Tom Jones A&P 110011000

FEDERAL AVIATION AGENCY **MAJOR REPAIR AND ALTERATION** **(Airframe, Powerplant, Propeller, or Appliance)**	*Form Approved Budget Bureau No. 04-R060.1* *FOR FAA USE ONLY* OFFICE IDENTIFICATION

INSTRUCTIONS: Print or type all entries. See FAR 43.9, FAR 43 Appendix B, and AC 43.9-1 (or subsequent revision thereof) for instructions and disposition of this form.

1. AIRCRAFT	MAKE: Cessna	MODEL: 172 K
	SERIAL NO.: 1234568	NATIONALITY AND REGISTRATION MARK: N 00110
2. OWNER	NAME *(As shown on registration certificate)*: John Doe	ADDRESS *(As shown on registration certificate)*: Box 00 Any town, WY

3. FOR FAA USE ONLY

4. UNIT IDENTIFICATION / **5. TYPE**

UNIT	MAKE	MODEL	SERIAL NO.	REPAIR	ALTERATION
AIRFRAME	(As described in item 1 above)			x	
POWERPLANT					
PROPELLER					
APPLIANCE	TYPE MANUFACTURER				

6. CONFORMITY STATEMENT

A. AGENCY'S NAME AND ADDRESS	B. KIND OF AGENCY	C. CERTIFICATE NO.
Sam Jones RR 3 Somewhere, USA	[X] U.S. CERTIFICATED MECHANIC [ ] FOREIGN CERTIFICATED MECHANIC [ ] CERTIFICATED REPAIR STATION [ ] MANUFACTURER	A&P 000123456

D. I certify that the repair and/or alteration made to the unit(s) identified in item 4 above and described on the reverse or attachments hereto have been made in accordance with the requirements of Part 43 of the U.S. Federal Aviation Regulations and that the information furnished herein is true and correct to the best of my knowledge.

DATE	SIGNATURE OF AUTHORIZED INDIVIDUAL
June 0, 0000	Sam Jones

7. APPROVAL FOR RETURN TO SERVICE

Pursuant to the authority given persons specified below, the unit identified in item 4 was inspected in the manner prescribed by the Administrator of the Federal Aviation Agency and is [X] APPROVED [ ] REJECTED

BY					
[ ] FAA FLT. STANDARDS INSPECTOR	[ ] MANUFACTURER	[x] INSPECTION AUTHORIZATION	OTHER *(Specify)*
[ ] FAA DESIGNEE	[ ] REPAIR STATION	[ ] CANADIAN DEPARTMENT OF TRANSPORT INSPECTOR OF AIRCRAFT	

DATE OF APPROVAL OR REJECTION	CERTIFICATE OR DESIGNATION NO.	SIGNATURE OF AUTHORIZED INDIVIDUAL
June 0, 0000	00110001 IA	James R. Robards

FAA Form 337 (1-65) OBSOLETE PREVIOUS EDITION 0052-025-8000 (8320)

NOTE: This form is provided for instructional purposes only. Since it may change at anytime please refer to your local GADO office for an exact form.

NOTICE

Weight and balance or operating limitation changes shall be entered in the appropriate aircraft record. An alteration must be compatible with all previous alterations to assure continued conformity with the applicable airworthiness requirements.

8. **DESCRIPTION OF WORK ACCOMPLISHED** *(If more space is required, attach additional sheets. Identify with aircraft nationality and registration mark and date work completed.)*

1. Replace the firewall with a new firewall in accordance with Cessna structural repair manual, para. 3, figure 18, and procedures and practices outlined in Section, 3, Chapter 2 of AC 43.13-1A.

---------------------------------end---------------------------------------

☐ ADDITIONAL SHEETS ARE ATTACHED

© U.S. GOVERNMENT PRINTING OFFICE 1965 OF—761-748

APPENDIX A
AIRWORTHINESS DIRECTIVE RECORD

AIRWORTHINESS DIRECTIVE RECORD

AIRCRAFT MAKE: **MODEL:** **SERIAL NUMBER:** **N NUMBER:**

AD Number	Date of Revision	Subject	Date of Compliance	Total Time At Compliance	Method of Compliance	One Time	Recurring	Next Due Date/ Time	Name Signature Number
76-03-05	2-17-76	Bracket Installation	6-30-78	826 Hrs.	Install bracket i/a/w Para. b.	x			John Larson (signature) John Larson A&P 00110000
76-05-04	7-12-76	Stab. Attach. Inspection	6-26-78	1248 Hrs.	Inspected Stab. Attach i/a/w Para. a & b		x	2248 Hrs	Tom Jones (signature) Tom Jones A&P 110011000

APPENDIX B
AIRWORTHINESS DIRECTIVE WORK SHEET

AIRWORTHINESS DIRECTIVE WORK SHEET

AIRCRAFT MAKE: MODEL: SERIAL NUMBER: N NUMBER:

AD Number	Subject	One Time	Recurring	Method of Compliance	Date/ Time C/W	Next Due Date/ time	Applicable	Not Applicable	Remarks

APPENDIX C
FORM 337 — MAJOR ALTERATION AND REPAIR

FEDERAL AVIATION AGENCY **MAJOR REPAIR AND ALTERATION** **(Airframe, Powerplant, Propeller, or Appliance)**	*Form Approved* *Budget Bureau No. 04–R060.1* *FOR FAA USE ONLY* OFFICE IDENTIFICATION

INSTRUCTIONS: Print or type all entries. See FAR 43.9, FAR 43 Appendix B, and AC 43.9–1 (or subsequent revision thereof) for instructions and disposition of this form.

1. AIRCRAFT	MAKE Cessna	MODEL 172 K
	SERIAL NO. 1234568	NATIONALITY AND REGISTRATION MARK N 00110
2. OWNER	NAME *(As shown on registration certificate)* John Doe	ADDRESS *(As shown on registration certificate)* Box 00 Any town, WY

3. FOR FAA USE ONLY

4. UNIT IDENTIFICATION				**5. TYPE**	
UNIT	MAKE	MODEL	SERIAL NO.	REPAIR	ALTERATION
AIRFRAME	(As described in item 1 above)			x	
POWERPLANT					
PROPELLER					
APPLIANCE	TYPE MANUFACTURER				

6. CONFORMITY STATEMENT

A. AGENCY'S NAME AND ADDRESS	B. KIND OF AGENCY	C. CERTIFICATE NO.
Sam Jones RR 3 Somewhere, USA	X U.S. CERTIFICATED MECHANIC ☐ FOREIGN CERTIFICATED MECHANIC ☐ CERTIFICATED REPAIR STATION ☐ MANUFACTURER	A&P 000123456

D. I certify that the repair and/or alteration made to the unit(s) identified in item 4 above and described on the reverse or attachments hereto have been made in accordance with the requirements of Part 43 of the U.S. Federal Aviation Regulations and that the information furnished herein is true and correct to the best of my knowledge.

DATE	SIGNATURE OF AUTHORIZED INDIVIDUAL
June 0, 0000	Sam Jones

7. APPROVAL FOR RETURN TO SERVICE

Pursuant to the authority given persons specified below, the unit identified in item 4 was inspected in the manner prescribed by the Administrator of the Federal Aviation Agency and is ☒ APPROVED ☐ REJECTED

BY				
☐ FAA FLT. STANDARDS INSPECTOR	☐ MANUFACTURER	x INSPECTION AUTHORIZATION	OTHER *(Specify)*
☐ FAA DESIGNEE	☐ REPAIR STATION	☐ CANADIAN DEPARTMENT OF TRANSPORT INSPECTOR OF AIRCRAFT	

DATE OF APPROVAL OR REJECTION	CERTIFICATE OR DESIGNATION NO.	SIGNATURE OF AUTHORIZED INDIVIDUAL
June 0, 0000	00110001 IA	James R. Robards

FAA Form 337 (1–65) OBSOLETE PREVIOUS EDITION 0052–025–8000 (8320)

NOTE: This form is provided for instructional purposes only. Since it may change at anytime please refer to your local GADO office for an exact form.

NOTICE

Weight and balance or operating limitation changes shall be entered in the appropriate aircraft record. An alteration must be compatible with all previous alterations to assure continued conformity with the applicable airworthiness requirements.

8. **DESCRIPTION OF WORK ACCOMPLISHED** *(If more space is required, attach additional sheets. Identify with aircraft nationality and registration mark and date work completed.)*

1. Replace the firewall with a new firewall in accordance with Cessna structural repair manual, para. 3, figure 18, and procedures and practices outlined in Section, 3, Chapter 2 of AC 43.13-1A.

----------------------------------end--

☐ ADDITIONAL SHEETS ARE ATTACHED

U S GOVERNMENT PRINTING OFFICE 1965 OF—761-748

[§ 43.9 Content, form, and disposition of maintenance, preventive maintenance, rebuilding, and alteration records (except inspections performed in accordance with Part 91, Part 123, Part 125, § 135.411(a)(1), and § 135.419 of this chapter).

[(a) *Maintenance record entries.* Except as provided in paragraphs (b) and (c) of this section, each person who maintains, performs preventive maintenance, rebuilds, or alters an aircraft, airframe, aircraft engine, propeller, appliance, or component part shall make an entry in the maintenance record of that equipment containing the following information:

[(1) A description (or reference to data acceptable to the Administrator) of work performed.

[(2) The date of completion of the work performed.

[(3) The name of the person performing the work if other than the person specified in paragraph (a) (4) of this section.

[(4) If the work performed on the aircraft, airframe, aircraft engine, propeller, appliance, or component part has been performed satisfactorily, the signature, certificate number, and kind of certificate held by the person approving the work. The signature constitutes the approval for return to service only for the work performed.

[In addition to the entry required by this paragraph, major repairs and major alterations shall be entered on a form, and the form disposed of, in the manner prescribed in Appendix B, by the person performing the work.

[(b) Each holder of an air carrier operating certificate or an operating certificate issued under Part 121, 127, or 135, that is required by its approved operations specifications to provide for a continuous airworthiness maintenance program, shall make a record of the maintenance, preventive maintenance, rebuilding, and alteration, on aircraft, airframes, aircraft engines, propellers, appliances, or component parts which it operates in accordance with the applicable provisions of Part 121, 127, or 135 of this chapter, as appropriate.

[(c) This section does not apply to persons performing inspections in accordance with Part 91, 123, 125, § 135.411(a) (1), or § 135.419 of this chapter.

[§ 43.11 Content, form, and disposition of the records for inspections conducted under Parts 91, 123, 125, § 135.411(a) (1), and § 135.419 of this chapter.

[(a) *Maintenance record entries.* The person approving or disapproving for return to service an aircraft, airframe, aircraft engine, propeller, appliance, or component part after any inspection performed in accordance with Part 91, 123, 125, § 135.411(a) (1), or § 135.419 shall make an entry in the maintenance record of that equipment containing the following information:

[(1) The type of inspection and a brief description of the extent of the inspection.

[(2) The date of the inspection and aircraft total time in service.

[(3) The signature, the certificate number, and kind of certificate held by the person approving or disapproving for return to service the aircraft, airframe, aircraft engine, propeller, appliance, component part, or portions thereof.

[(4) Except for progressive inspections, if the aircraft is found to be airworthy and approved for return to service, the following or a similarly worded statement—"I certify that this aircraft has been inspected in accordance with (insert type) inspection and was determined to be in airworthy condition."

[(5) Except for progressive inspections, if the aircraft is not approved for return to service because of needed maintenance, noncompliance with applicable specifications, airworthiness directives, or other approved data, the following or a similarly worded statement—"I certify that this aircraft has been inspected in accordance with (insert type) inspection and a list of discrepancies and unairworthy items dated (date) has been provided for the aircraft owner or operator."

[(6) For progressive inspections, the following or a similarly worded statement—"I certify that in accordance with a progressive inspection program, a routine inspection of (identify whether aircraft or components) and a detailed inspection of (identify components) were performed and the (aircraft or components) are (approved or disapproved) for return to service." If disapproved, the entry will further state "and a list of discrepancies and unairworthy items dated (date) has been provided to the aircraft owner or operator."

[(7) If an inspection is conducted under an inspection program provided for in Part 91, 123, 125, or § 135.411(a) (1), the entry must identify the inspection program, that part of the inspection program accomplished, and contain a statement that the inspection was performed in accordance with the inspections and procedures for that particular program.

[(b) *Listing of discrepancies.* If the person performing any inspection required by Part 91, 123, 125, or § 135.411(a) (1) of this chapter finds that the aircraft is unairworthy or does not meet the applicable type certificate data, airworthiness directives, or other approved data upon which its airworthiness depends, that person must give the owner or lessee a signed and dated list of those discrepancies.]

§ 43.12 Maintenance records: falsification, reproduction, or alteration.

(a) No person may make or cause to be made:

[(1) Any fraudulent or intentionally false entry in any record or report that is required to be made, kept, or used to show compliance with any requirement under this Part;]

(2) Any reproduction, for fraudulent purpose, of any record or report under this Part; or

(3) Any alteration, for fraudulent purpose, of any record or report under this Part.

(b) The commission by any person of an act prohibited under paragraph (a) of this section is a basis for suspending or revoking the applicable airman, operator, or production certificate, Technical Standard Order Authorization, FAA-Parts Manufacturer Approval, or Product and Process Specification issued by the Administrator and held by that person.

APPENDIX E

FAR 43, APPENDIX D — INSPECTION ITEMS

Scope and Detail of Items (as Applicable to the Particular Aircraft) to be Included in Annual and 100–Hour Inspections

(a) Each person performing an annual or 100-hour inspection shall, before that inspection, remove or open all necessary inspection plates, access doors, fairing, and cowling. He shall thoroughly clean the aircraft and aircraft engine.

(b) Each person performing an annual or 100-hour inspection shall inspect (where applicable) the following components of the fuselage and hull group:

(1) Fabric and skin—for deterioration, distortion, other evidence of failure, and defective or insecure attachment of fittings.

(2) Systems and components—for improper installation, apparent defects, and unsatisfactory operation.

(3) Envelope, gas bags, ballast tanks, and related parts—for poor condition.

(c) Each person performing an annual or 100-hour inspection shall inspect (where applicable) the following components of the cabin and cockpit group:

(1) Generally—for uncleanliness and loose equipment that might foul the controls.

(2) Seats and safety belts—for poor condition and apparent defects.

(3) Windows and windshields—for deterioration and breakage.

(4) Instruments—for poor condition, mounting, marking, and (where practicable) for improper operation.

(5) Flight and engine controls—for improper installation and improper operation.

(6) Batteries—for improper installation and improper charge.

(7) All systems—for improper installation, poor general condition, apparent and obvious defects, and insecurity of attachment.

(d) Each person performing an annual or 100-hour inspection shall inspect (where applicable) components of the engine and nacelle group as follows:

(1) Engine section—for visual evidence of excessive oil, fuel, or hydraulic leaks, and sources of such leaks.

(2) Studs and nuts—for improper torquing and obvious defects.

(3) Internal engine—for cylinder compression and for metal particles or foreign matter on screens and sump drain plugs. If there is weak cylinder compression, for improper internal condition and improper internal tolerances.

(4) Engine mount—for cracks, looseness of mounting, and looseness of engine to mount.

(5) Flexible vibration dampeners—for poor condition and deterioration.

(6) Engine controls—for defects, improper travel, and improper safetying.

(7) Lines, hoses, and clamps—for leaks, improper condition, and looseness.

(8) Exhaust stacks—for cracks, defects, and improper attachment.

(9) Accessories—for apparent defects in security of mounting.

(10) All systems—for improper installation, poor general condition, defects, and insecure attachment.

(11) Cowling—for cracks, and defects.

(e) Each person performing an annual or 100-hour inspection shall inspect (where applicable) the following components of the landing gear group:

(1) All units—for poor condition and insecurity of attachment.

(2) Shock absorbing devices—for improper oleo fluid level.

(3) Linkage, trusses, and members—for undue or excessive wear, fatigue, and distortion.

(4) Retracting and locking mechanism—for improper operation.

(5) Hydraulic lines—for leakage.

(6) Electrical system—for chafing and improper operation of switches.

(7) Wheels—for cracks, defects, and condition of bearings.

(8) Tires—for wear and cuts.

(9) Brakes—for improper adjustment.

(10) Floats and skis—for insecure attachment and obvious or apparent defects.

(f) Each person performing an annual or 100-hour inspection shall inspect (where applicable) all components of the wing and center section assembly for poor general condition, fabric or skin deterioration, distortion, evidence of failure, and insecurity of attachment.

(g) Each person performing an annual or 100-hour inspection shall inspect (where applicable) all components and systems that make up the complete empennage assembly for poor general condition, fabric or skin deterioration, distortion, evidence of failure, insecure attachment, improper component installation, and improper component operation.

(h) Each person performing an annual or 100-hour inspection shall inspect (where applicable) the following components of the propeller group:

(1) Propeller assembly—for cracks, nicks, binds, and oil leakage.

(2) Bolts—for improper torquing and lack of safetying.

(3) Anti-icing devices—for improper operations and obvious defects.

(4) Control mechanisms—for improper operation, insecure mounting, and restricted travel.

(i) Each person performing an annual or 100-hour inspection shall inspect (where applicable) the following components of the radio group:

(1) Radio and electronic equipment—for improper installation and insecure mounting.

(2) Wiring and conduits—for improper routing, insecure mounting, and obvious defects.

(3) Bonding and shielding—for improper installation and poor condition.

(4) Antenna including trailing antenna—for poor condition, insecure mounting, and improper operation.

(j) Each person performing an annual or 100-hour inspection shall inspect (where applicable) each installed miscellaneous item that is not otherwise covered by this listing for improper installation and improper operation.

§ 91.169 Inspections.

(a) Except as provided in paragraph (c) of this section, no person may operate an aircraft unless, within the preceding 12 calendar months, it has had—

(1) An annual inspection in accordance with Part 43 of this chapter and has been approved for return to service by a person authorized by § 43.7 of this chapter; or

(2) An inspection for the issue of an airworthiness certificate.

No inspection performed under paragraph (b) of the section may be substituted for any inspection required by this paragraph unless it is performed by a person authorized to perform annual inspections, and is entered as an 'annual' inspection in the required maintenance records.

(b) Except as provided in paragraph (c) of this section, no person may operate an aircraft carrying any person (other than a crewmember) for hire, and no person may give flight instruction for hire in an aircraft which that person provides, unless within the preceding 100 hours of time in service it has received an annual or 100-hour inspection and been approved for return to service in accordance with Part 43 of this chapter, or received an inspection for the issuance of an airworthiness certificate in accordance with Part 21 of this chapter. The 100-hour limitation may be exceeded by not more than 10 hours if necessary to reach a place at which the inspection can be done. The excess time, however, is included in computing the next 100 hours of time in service.

[(c) Paragraphs (a) and (b) of this section do not apply to—

[(1) An aircraft that carries a special flight permit, a current experimental certificate, or a provisional airworthiness certificate;

[(2) An aircraft inspected in accordance with an approved aircraft inspection program under Part 123, 125, or 135 of this chapter and so identified by the registration number in the operations specifications of the certificate holder having the approved inspection program; or

[(3) An aircraft subject to the requirements of paragraph (d) or (e) of this section.

[(d) *Progressive inspection.* Each registered owner or operator of an aircraft desiring to use a progressive inspection program must submit a written request to the FAA Flight Standards district office having jurisdiction over the area in which the applicant is located, and shall provide—

[(1) A certificated mechanic holding an inspection authorization, a certificated airframe repair station, or the manufacturer of the aircraft to supervise or conduct the progressive inspection;

[(2) A current inspection procedures manual available and readily understandable to pilot and maintenance personnel containing, in detail—

[(i) An explanation of the progressive inspection, including the continuity of inspection responsibility, the making of reports, and the keeping of records and technical reference material;

[(ii) An inspection schedule, specifying the intervals in hours or days when routine and detailed inspections will be performed and including instructions for exceeding an inspection interval by not more than 10 hours while en route and for changing an inspection interval because of service experience;

[(iii) Sample routine and detailed inspection forms and instructions for their use; and

[(iv) Sample reports and records and instructions for their use;

[(3) Enough housing and equipment for necessary disassembly and proper inspection of the aircraft; and

[(4) Appropriate current technical information for the aircraft.

[The frequency and detail of the progressive inspection shall provide for the complete inspection of the aircraft within each 12-calendar months and be consistent with the manufacturer's recommendations, field service experience, and the kind of operation in which the aircraft is engaged. The progressive inspection schedule must ensure that the aircraft, at all times, will be airworthy and will conform to all applicable FAA aircraft specifications, type certificate data sheets, airworthiness directives, and other approved data. If the progressive inspection is discontinued, the owner or operator shall immediately notify the local FAA Flight Standards district office, in writing, of the discontinuance. After the discontinuance, the first annual inspection under § 91.169(a) is due within 12 calendar months after the last complete inspection of the aircraft under the progressive inspection. The 100-hour inspection under § 91.169(b) is due within 100 hours after that complete inspection. A complete inspection of the aircraft, for the purpose of determining when the annual and 100-hour inspections are due, requires a detailed inspection of the aircraft and all its components in accordance with the progressive inspection. A routine inspection of the aircraft and a detailed inspection of several components is not considered to be a complete inspection.

[(e) *Large airplanes (to which Part 125 is not applicable), turbojet multiengine airplanes, and turbopropeller-powered multiengine airplanes.* No person may operate a large airplane, turbojet multiengine airplane, or turbopropeller-powered multiengine airplane unless the replacement times for life-limited parts specified in the aircraft specifications, type data sheets, or other documents approved by the Administrator are complied with and the airplane, including the airframe engines, propellers, appliances, survival equipment, and emergency equipment, is inspected in accordance with an inspection program selected under the provisions of paragraph (f) of this section.

[(f) *Selection of inspection programs under paragraph (e) of this section.* The registered owner or operator of each airplane described in paragraph (e) of this section must select, identify in the aircraft maintenance records, and use one of the following programs for the inspection of that airplane:

[(1) A continuous airworthiness inspection program that is part of a continuous airworthiness maintenance program currently in use by a person holding an air carrier operating certificate or an operating certificate issued under Part 121, 127, or 135 of this chapter and operating that make and model airplane under Part 121 or 127 or operating that make and model under Part 135 and maintaining it under § 135.411(a) (2).

[(2) An approved aircraft inspection program approved under § 135.419 of this chapter and currently in use by a person holding an operating certificate issued under Part 135.

[(3) An approved continuous inspection program currently in use by a person certificated under Part 123 of this chapter.

[(4) A current inspection program recommended by the manufacturer.

[(5) Any other inspection program established by the registered owner or operator of that airplane and approved by the Administrator under paragraph (g) of this section. However, the Administrator may require revision to this inspection program in accordance with the provisions of § 91.170.

[Each operator shall include in the selected program the name and address of the person responsible for scheduling the inspections required by the program and make a copy of that program available to the person performing inspections on the airplane and, upon request, to the Administrator.

[(g) *Inspection program approval under paragraph (e) of this section.* Each operator of an airplane desiring to establish or change an approved inspection program under paragraph (f) (5) of this section must submit the program for approval to the local FAA Flight Standards district office having jurisdiction over the area in which the airplane is based. The program must be in writing and include at least the following information:

[(1) Instruction and procedures for the conduct of inspections for the particular make and model airplane, including necessary tests and checks. The instructions and procedures must set forth in detail the parts and areas of the airframe, engines, propellers, and appliances, including survival and emergency equipment required to be inspected.

[(2) A schedule for performing the inspections that must be performed under the program expressed in terms of the time in service, calendar time, number of system operations, or any combination of these.

[(h) *Changes from one inspection program to another.* When an operator changes from one inspection program under paragraph (f) of this section to another, the time in service, calendar times, or cycles of operation accumulated under the previous program must be applied in determining inspection due times under the new program.]

U.S. Department of Transportation
Federal Aviation Administration

Advisory Circular

Subject: MAINTENANCE RECORDS **Date:** 1/9/84 **Initiated by:** AWS-340 **AC No:** 43-9B **Change:**

1. PURPOSE. This advisory circular (AC) discusses maintenance record requirements under Federal Aviation Regulations (FAR) Part 43, Sections 43.9, 43.11, Part 91, Section 91.173, and the related responsibilities of owners, operators, and persons performing maintenance, preventive maintenance, and alterations.

2. CANCELLATION. AC 43-9A, Maintenance Records: General Aviation Aircraft, dated September 9, 1977, is cancelled.

3. RELATED FAR'S. FAR Parts 1, 43, 91, and 145.

4. BACKGROUND. The maintenance record requirements of Parts 43 and 91 have remained essentially the same for several years. Certain areas, however, continue to be misunderstood and changes to both Parts have recently been made. Those misunderstood areas and the recent changes necessitate this reiteration of Federal Aviation Administration (FAA) policy and an explanation of the changes.

5. DISCUSSION. Proper management of an aircraft operation begins with, and depends upon, a good maintenance record system. Properly executed and retained records provide owners, operators, and maintenance persons information essential in: controlling scheduled and unscheduled maintenance; evaluating the quality of maintenance sources; evaluating the economics and procedures of maintenance programs; troubleshooting; and eliminating the need for reinspection and/or rework to establish airworthiness. Only that information required to be a part of the maintenance record should be included and retained. Voluminous and irrelevant entries reduce the value of records in meeting their purposes.

6. MAINTENANCE RECORD REQUIREMENTS.

a. Responsibilities. Aircraft maintenance recordkeeping is a responsibility shared by the owner/operator and maintenance persons, with the ultimate responsibility assigned to the owner/operator by FAR Part 91, Section 91.165. Sections 91.165 and 91.173 set forth the requirements for owners and operators, while FAR Part 43, Sections 43.9 and 43.11 contain the requirements for maintenance persons. In general, the requirements for owners/operators and maintenance persons are the same; however, some small differences exist. These differences are discussed in this AC under the rule in which they exist.

b. Maintenance Record Entries Required. Section 91.165 requires each owner or operator to ensure that maintenance persons make appropriate entries in the maintenance records to indicate the aircraft has been approved for return to service. Thus, the prime responsibility for maintenance records lies with the owner or operator. Section 43.9(a) requires persons performing maintenance, preventive maintenance, rebuilding, or alteration to make entries in the maintenance record of the equipment worked on. Maintenance persons, therefore, share the responsibility for maintenance records.

c. Maintenance Records are to be Retained. Section 91.173(a) sets forth the minimum content requirements and retention requirements for maintenance records. Maintenance records may be kept in any format which provides record continuity, includes required contents, lends itself to the addition of new entries, provides for signature entry, and is not confusing. Section 91.173(b) requires records of maintenance, alteration, and required or approved inspections to be retained until the work is repeated, superseded by other work, or for 1 year. It also requires the records, specified in Section 91.173(a)(2), to be retained and transferred with the aircraft at the time of sale.

NOTE: Section 91.173(a) contains an exception regarding work accomplished in accordance with Section 91.171. This does not exclude the making of entries for this work, but applies to the retention period of the records for work done in accordance with this section. The exclusion is necessary since the retention period of 1 year is inconsistent with the 24-month interval of test and inspection specified in Section 91.171. Entries for work done per this section are to be retained for 24 months or until the work is repeated or superseded.

d. Section 91.173(a)(1). This section requires a record of maintenance, for each aircraft (including the airframe) and each engine, propeller, rotor, and appliance of an aircraft. This does not require separate or individual records for each of these items. It does require the information specified in Sections 91.173(a)(1) through 91.173(a)(2)(vi) to be kept for each item as appropriate. As a practical matter, many owners and operators find it advantageous to keep separate or individual records since it facilitates transfer of the record with the item when ownership changes. Section 91.173(a)(1) has no counterpart in Section 43.9 or Section 43.11.

e. Section 91.173(a)(1)(i). This section requires the maintenance record entry to include "a description of the work performed." The description should be in sufficient detail to permit a person unfamiliar with the work to understand what was done, and the methods and procedures used in doing it. When the work is extensive, this results in a voluminous record and involves considerable time. To provide for this contingency, the rule permits reference to technical data acceptable to the Administrator in lieu of making the detailed entry. Manufacturer's manuals, service letters, bulletins, work orders, FAA advisory circulars, Major Repair and Alteration Forms (FAA Form 337), and others, which accurately describe what was done, or how it was done, may be referenced. Except for the documents mentioned, which are in common usage, referenced documents are to be made a part of the maintenance records and retained in accordance with Section 91.173(b). Certificated repair stations frequently work on components shipped to them when, as a consequence, the maintenance records are unavailable. To provide for this situation, repair stations should supply owners and operators with copies of work orders written for the work, in lieu of maintenance record entries. The work order copy must include the information required by Section 91.173(a)(1) through Section 91.173(a)(1)(iii), be made a part of the maintenance record, and retained per Section 91.173(b). This procedure is not the same as that for maintenance releases discussed in paragraph 17 of this AC, and it may not be used when maintenance records are available. Section 91.173(a)(1)(i) is identical to it's counterpart, Section 43.9(a)(1), which imposes the same requirements on maintenance persons.

f. Section 91.173(a)(1)(ii) is identical to Section 43.9(a)(2) and requires entries to contain the date the work accomplished was completed. This is normally the date upon which the work is approved for return to service. However, when work is accomplished by one person and approved for return to service by another, the dates may differ. Two signatures may also appear under this circumstance; however, a single entry in accordance with Section 43.9(a)(3) is acceptable.

g. Section 91.173(a)(1)(iii) differs slightly from Section 43.9(a)(4) in that it requires the entry to indicate only the signature and certificate number of the person approving the work for return to service, and does not require the type of certificate being exercised to be indicated as does Section 43.9(a)(4). This is a new requirement of Section 43.9(a)(4), which assists owners and operators in meeting their responsibilities. Maintenance persons may indicate the type of certificate exercised by using A, P, A&P, IA, or RS for mechanic with airframe rating, with powerplant rating, with both ratings, with inspection authorization, or repair station, respectively.

h. Section 91.173(a)(2) requires six items to be made a part of the maintenance record and maintained as such. Section 43.9 does not require maintenance persons to enter these items. Section 43.11 requires some of them to be part of entries made for inspections, but they are all the responsibility of the owner or operator. The six items are discussed as follows:

(1) Section 91.173(a)(2)(i) requires a record of total time in service to be kept for the airframe, each engine, and each propeller. FAR Part 1, Section 1.1, Definitions, defines "time in service," with respect to maintenance time records, as that time from the moment an aircraft leaves the surface of the earth until it touches it at the next point of landing. Section 43.9 does not require this to be part of the entries for maintenance, preventive maintenance, rebuilding, or alterations. However, Section 43.11 requires maintenance persons to make it a part of the entries for inspections made under Parts 91, 125, and Sections 135.411(a)(1) and 135.419. It is good practice to include time in service in all entries.

(i) Some circumstances impact the owner's or operator's ability to comply with Section 91.173(a)(2)(i). For example: in the case of rebuilt engines, the owner or operator would not have a way of knowing the "total time in service," since Section 91.175 permits the maintenance record to be discontinued and the engine time to be started at "zero." In this case, the maintenance record and "time in service," subsequent to the rebuild, comprise a satisfactory record.

(ii) Many components, presently in service, were put into service prior to the requirements to keep maintenance records on them. Propellers are probably foremost in this group. In these instances, practicable procedures for compliance with the record requirements must be used. For example: "total time in service" may be derived using the procedures described in paragraph 13, Lost or Destroyed Records, of this AC; or if records prior to the regulatory requirements are just not available from any source, "time in service" may be kept since last complete overhaul. Neither of these procedures is acceptable when life-limited-parts status is involved or when AD compliance is a factor. Only the actual record since new may be used in these instances.

(iii) Sometimes engines are assembled from modules (turbojet and some turbopropeller engines) and a true "total time in service" for the total engine is not kept. If owners and operators wish to take advantage of this modular design, then "total time in service" and a maintenance record for each module is to be maintained. The maintenance records specified in Section 91.173(a)(2) are to be kept with the module.

(2) Section 91.173(a)(2)(ii) requires the current status of life-limited parts to be part of the maintenance record. If "total time in service" of the aircraft, engine, propeller, etc., is entered in the record when a life-limited part is installed and the "time in service" of the life-limited part is included, the normal record of time in service automatically meets this requirement.

(3) Section 91.173(a)(2)(iii) requires the maintenance record to indicate the time since last overhaul of all items installed on the aircraft which are required to be overhauled on a specified time basis. The explanation in paragraph 6h(2) of this AC also applies to this requirement.

(4) Section 91.173(a)(2)(iv) deals with the current inspection status and requires it to be reflected in the maintenance record. Again, the explanation in paragraph 6h(2) is appropriate even though Section 43.11(a)(2) requires maintenance persons to determine "time in service" of the item being inspected and to include it as part of the inspection entry.

(5) Section 91.173(a)(2)(v) requires the current status of applicable airworthiness directives (AD) to be a part of the maintenance record. The record is to include, at minimum, the method used to comply with the AD, the AD number, and revision date; and if the AD has requirements for recurring action, the time in service and the date when that action is required. When AD's are accomplished, maintenance persons are required to include the items specified in Section 43.9(a)(2),(3), and (4) in addition to those required by Section 91.173(a)(2)(v). An example of a maintenance record format for AD compliance is contained in Appendix 1 of this AC.

(6) Section 91.173(a)(2)(vi). In the past, the owner or operator has been permitted to maintain a list of current major alterations to the airframe, engine(s), propeller(s), rotor(s), or appliances. This procedure did not produce a record of value to the owner/operator or to maintenance persons in determining the continued airworthiness of the alteration since such a record was not sufficient detail. This section of the rule has now been changed. It now prescribes that copies of the FAA Form 337, issued for the alteration, be made a part of the maintenance record.

7. PREVENTIVE MAINTENANCE.

a. Preventive maintenance is defined in Part 1, Section 1.1. Part 43, Appendix A, paragraph (c) lists those items which a pilot may accomplish under Section 43.3(g). Section 43.7 authorizes appropriately rated repair stations and mechanics, and persons holding at least a private pilot certificate to approve an aircraft for return to service after they have performed preventive maintenance. All of these persons must record preventive maintenance accomplished in accordance with the requirements of Section 43.9. Advisory Circular (AC)43-12, Preventive Maintenance, (as revised) contains further information on this subject.

b. The type of certificate exercised when maintenance or preventive maintenance is accomplished must be indicated in the maintenance record. Pilots may use PP, CP, or ATP to indicate private, commercial, or airline transport pilot certificate, respectively in approving preventive maintenance for return to service. Pilots are not authorized by Section 43.3(g) to perform preventive maintenance on aircraft when they are operated under Parts 121, 127, 129, or 135. Pilots may only approve for return to service preventive maintenance which they themselves have accomplished.

8. REBUILT ENGINE MAINTENANCE RECORDS.

a. Section 91.175 provides that "zero time" may be granted to an engine that has been rebuilt by a manufacturer or an agency approved by the manufacturer. When this is done, the owner/operator may use a new maintenance record without regard to previous operating history.

b. The manufacturer or an agency approved by the manufacturer that rebuilds and grants zero time to an engine is required by Section 91.175 to provide a signed statement containing: (1) the date the engine was rebuilt; (2) each change made as required by an AD; and (3) each change made in compliance with service bulletins, when the service bulletin specifically requests an entry to be made.

c. Section 43.2(b) prohibits the use of the term "rebuilt" in describing work accomplished in required maintenance records or forms unless the component worked on has had specific work functions accomplished. These functions are listed in Section 43.2(b) and, except for testing requirements, are the same as those set forth in Section 91.175. When terms such as "remanufactured," "reconditioned," or other terms coined by various aviation enterprises are used in maintenance records, owners and operators cannot assume that the functions outlined in Section 43.2(b) have been done.

9. RECORDING TACHOMETERS.

a. Time-in-service recording devices. These devices sense such things as: electrical power on, oil pressure, wheels on the ground, etc., and from these conditions provide an indication of time in service. With the exception of those which sense aircraft liftoff and touchdown, the indications are approximate.

b. Some owners and operators mistakenly believe these devices may be used in lieu of keeping time in service in the maintenance record. While they are of great assistance in arriving at time in service, such instruments, alone, do not meet the requirements of Section 91.173. For example, when the device fails and requires change, it is necessary to enter time in service and the instrument reading at the change. Otherwise, record continuity is lost.

10. MAINTENANCE RECORDS FOR AD COMPLIANCE. This subject is covered in AC 39-7, Airworthiness Directives for General Aviation Aircraft, as revised. A separate record may be kept for the airframe and each engine, propeller, rotor, and appliance, but is not required. This would facilitate record searches when inspection is needed, and when an engine, propeller, rotor, or appliance is removed, the record may be transferred with it. Such records may also be used as a schedule for recurring inspections. The format, shown in Appendix 1, is a suggested one, and adherence is not mandatory. Owners should be aware that they may be responsible for noncompliance with AD's when their aircraft are leased to foreign operators. They should, therefore, ensure that AD's are passed on to all their foreign lessees, and leases should be drafted to deal with this subject.

11. MAINTENANCE RECORDS FOR REQUIRED INSPECTIONS.

a. Section 43.11 contains the requirements for inspection entries. While these requirements are imposed on maintenance persons, owners and operators should become familiar with them in order to meet their responsibilities under Section 91.165.

b. The maintenance record requirements of Section 43.11 apply to the 100-hour, annual, and progressive inspections under Part 91; continuous inspection programs under Parts 91 and 125; Approved Airplane Inspection Programs under Part 135; and the 100-hour and annual inspections under Section 135.411(a)(1).

c. Misunderstandings persist regarding entry requirements for inspections under Section 91.169(e) (formerly Section 91.217). These requirements were formerly found in Section 43.9(a) and this contributed to misunderstanding. Appropriately rated mechanics without an inspection authorization (IA) are authorized to conduct these inspections and make the required entries. Particular attention should be given to Section 43.11(a)(7) in that it now requires a more specific statement than that previously required under Section 43.9. The entry, in addition to other items, must identify the inspection program used; identify the portion or segment of the inspection program accomplished; and contain a statement that the inspection was performed in accordance with the instructions and procedures for that program.

d. Questions continue regarding multiple entries for 100-hour/annual inspections. As discussed in paragraph 6d of this AC, neither Part 43 nor Part 91 requires separate records to be kept. Section 43.11, however, requires persons approving or disapproving equipment for return to service, after any required inspection, to make an entry in the record of that equipment. Therefore, when an owner maintains a single record, the entry of the 100-hour or annual inspection is made in that record. If the owner maintains separate records for the airframe, powerplants, and propellers, the entry for the 100-hour or annual inspection is entered in each.

12. DISCREPANCY LISTS.

a. Prior to October 15, 1982, issuance of discrepancy lists (or lists of defects) to owners or operators was appropriate only in connection with annual inspections under Part 91; inspections under Section 135.411(a)(1) of Part 135; continuous inspection programs under Part 125; and inspections under Section 91.217 of Part 91. Now, Section 43.11 requires that a discrepancy list be prepared by a person performing any inspection required by Parts 91, 125, or Section 135.411(a)(1) of Part 135.

b. When a discrepancy list is provided to an owner or operator, it says in effect, "except for these discrepancies, the item inspected is airworthy." It is imperative, therefore, that inspections be complete and that all discrepancies appear in the list. When circumstances dictate that an inspection be terminated before it is completed, the maintenance record should clearly indicate that the inspection was discontinued. The entry should meet all the other requirements of Section 43.11.

c. It is no longer a requirement that copies of discrepancy lists be forwarded to the local FAA District Office.

d. Discrepancy lists (or lists of defects) are part of the maintenance record and the owner/operator is responsible to maintain that record in accordance with Section 91.173(b)(3). The entry made by maintenance persons in the maintenance record should reference the discrepancy list when a list is issued.

13. LOST OR DESTROYED RECORDS. Occasionally, the records for an aircraft are lost or destroyed. This can create a considerable problem in reconstructing the aircraft records. First, it is necessary to reestablish the total time in service of the airframe. This can be done by: reference to other records which reflect the time in service; research of records maintained by repair facilities; and reference to records maintained by individual mechanics, etc. When these things have been done and the record is still incomplete, the owner/operator may make a notarized statement in the new record describing the loss and establishing the time in service based on the research and the best estimate of time in service.

a. The current status of applicable AD's may present a more formidable problem. This may require a detailed inspection by maintenance personnel to establish that the applicable AD's have been complied with. It can readily be seen that this could entail considerable time, expense and, in some instances, might require recompliance with the AD.

b. Other items required by Section 91.173(a)(2), such as the current status of life-limited parts, time since last overhaul, current inspection status, and current list of major alterations, may present difficult problems. Some items may be easier to reestablish than others, but all are problems. Losing maintenance records can be troublesome, costly, and time consuming. Safekeeping of the records is an integral part of a good record system.

14. COMPUTERIZED RECORDS. There is a growing trend toward computerized maintenance records. Many of these systems are offered to owners/operators on a commercial basis. While these are excellent scheduling systems, alone, they normally do not meet the requirements of Sections 43.9 or 91.173. The owner/operator who uses such a system is required to ensure that it provides the information required by Section 91.173, including signatures. If not, modification to make them complete is the owners/operators responsibility and the responsibility may not be delegated.

15. PUBLIC AIRCRAFT. Prospective purchasers of aircraft, that have been used as public aircraft, should be aware that public aircraft are not subject to the certification and maintenance requirements in the FAR's and may not have records which meet the requirements of Section 91.173. Considerable research may be involved in establishing the required records when these aircraft are purchased and brought into civil aviation. The aircraft may not be certificated or used without such records.

16. LIFE-LIMITED PARTS.

a. Present day aircraft and powerplants commonly have life-limited parts installed. These life limits may be referred to as retirement times, service life limitations, parts retirement limitations, retirement life limits, life limitations, or other such terminology and may be expressed in hours, cycles of operation, or calendar time. They are set forth in type certificate data sheets, AD's, and operator's operations specifications, FAA-approved maintenance programs, the limitations section of FAA-approved airplane or rotorcraft flight manuals, and manuals required by operating rules.

b. Section 91.173(a)(2)(ii) requires the owner or operator of an aircraft with such parts installed to have records containing the current status of these parts. Many owners/operators have found it advantageous to have a separate record for such parts showing the name of the part, part number, serial number, date of installation, total time in service, date removed, and signature and certificate number of the person installing or removing the part. A separate record, as described, facilitates transferring the record with the part in the event the part is removed and later reinstalled or installed on another aircraft or engine. If a separate record is not kept, the aircraft record must contain sufficient information to clearly establish the status of the life-limited parts installed.

17. MAINTENANCE RELEASE.

a. In addition to those requirements discussed previously in this AC, Section 43.9 requires that major repairs and alterations be recorded as indicated in Appendix B of Part 43, (i.e., on FAA Form 337). An exception is provided in paragraph (b) of that appendix which allows repair stations certificated under Part 145 to use a maintenance release in lieu of the form for major repairs (and only major repairs).

b. The maintenance release must contain the information specified in paragraph (b)(3) of Appendix B of Part 43, be made a part of the aircraft maintenance record, and retained by the owner/operator as specified in Section 91.173. The maintenance release is usually a special document (normally a tag) and is attached to the product when it is approved for return to service. The maintenance release may, however, be on a copy of the work order written for the product. When this is done (it may be used only for major repairs) the entry on the work order must meet paragraph (b)(3) of the appendix.

c. Some repair stations use what they call a maintenance release for other than major repairs. This is sometimes a tag and sometimes information on a work order. When this is done, all of the requirements of Section 43.9 must be met (those of (b)(3) of the appendix are not applicable) and the document is to be made and retained as part of the maintenance records under Section 91.173. This was discussed in paragraph 6e of this AC.

18. FAA FORM 337.

a. Major repairs and alterations are to be recorded on FAA Form 337, Major Repair and Alteration, as stated in paragraph 17. This form is executed by the person making the repair or alteration. Provisions are made on the form for a person other than that person performing the work to approve the repair or alteration for return to service.

b. These forms are now required to be made part of the maintenance record of the product repaired or altered and retained in accordance with Section 91.173.

c. Detailed instructions for use of this form are contained in AC 43.9-1D, Instructions for Completion of FAA Form 337, Major Repair and Alteration.

d. Some manufacturers have initiated a policy of indicating, on their service letters and bulletins, and other documents dealing with changes to their aircraft, whether or not the changes constitute major repairs or alterations. They also indicate when, in their opinion, a Form 337 lies with the person accomplishing the repairs or alterations and cannot be delegated. When there is a question, it is advisable to contact the local office of the FAA for guidance.

19. TESTS AND INSPECTIONS FOR ALTIMETER SYSTEMS, ALTITUDE REPORTING EQUIPMENT, AND ATC TRANSPONDERS. The recordation requirements for these tests and inspections are the same as for other maintenance. There are essentially three tests and inspections, (the altimeter system, the transponder system, and the data correspondence test) each of which may be subdivided relative to who may perform specific portions of the test. The basic authorization for performing these tests and inspections, found in Section 43.3, are supplemented by Sections 91.171 and 91.172. When multiple persons are involved in the performance of tests and inspections, care must be exercised to insure proper authorization under these three sections and compliance with Sections 43.9 and 43.9(a)(3) in particular.

20. BEFORE YOU BUY. This is the proper time to take a close look at the maintenance records of any used aircraft you expect to purchase. A well-kept set of maintenance records, which properly identifies all previously performed maintenance, alterations, and AD compliances, is generally a good indicator of the aircraft condition. This is not always the case, but in any event, before you buy, require the owner to produce the maintenance records for your examination, and require correction of any discrepancies found on the aircraft or in the records. Many prospective owners have found it advantageous to have a reliable unbiased maintenance person examine the maintenance records, as well as the aircraft, before negotiations have progressed too far. If the aircraft is purchased, take the time to review and learn the system of the previous owner to ensure compliance and continuity when you modify or continue that system.

M. C. Beard
Director of Airworthiness

APPENDIX 1. AIRWORTHINESS DIRECTIVE COMPLIANCE RECORD (SUGGESTED FORMAT)

APPENDIX 1. AIRWORTHINESS DIRECTIVE COMPLIANCE RECORD

*Aircraft, Engine, Propeller, Rotor, or Appliance: Make_________ Model_________ Ser.No._________ N____________

AD Number and Amendment Number	Date Received	Subject	Compliance Due Date Hours/ Other	Method of Compliance	Date of Compliance	Airframe Total Time In Service at Compliance	Component Total Time In Service at Compliance	One-Time	Recur-ring	Next Comp. Due Date Hours/ Other	Authorized Signature, Certificate Type and Number	Remarks

*Suggest providing a page for each category.

AC 43.9-1D

DATE 9/5/79

ADVISORY CIRCULAR

DEPARTMENT OF TRANSPORTATION
Federal Aviation Administration
Washington, D.C.

FAR GUIDANCE MATERIAL

Subject: INSTRUCTIONS FOR COMPLETION OF FAA FORM 337 (OMB 04-R0060), MAJOR REPAIR AND ALTERATION (AIRFRAME, POWERPLANT, PROPELLER, OR APPLIANCE)

1. PURPOSE. This advisory circular (AC) provides instructions for completing FAA Form 337, Major Repair and Alteration (Airframe, Powerplant, Propeller, or Appliance).

2. CANCELLATION. AC 43.9-1C, Instructions for Completion of FAA Form 337 (OMB 04-R0060) Major Repair and Alteration (Airframe, Powerplant, Propeller or Appliance), dated 12/20/73, is canceled.

3. RELATED FAR SECTIONS. Federal Aviation Regulation (FAR) Part 43, Sections 43.5, 43.7, 43.9, and Appendix B.

4. INFORMATION. FAA Form 337 is furnished free of charge by the Federal Aviation Administration (FAA) and is available at all FAA Air Carrier, General Aviation, Engineering and Manufacturing, and Flight Standards District Offices and all International Field Offices. The form serves two main purposes; one is to provide aircraft owners and operators with a record of major repairs or alterations indicating details and approval, and the other is to provide the FAA with a copy of the form for inclusion in the aircraft records at the FAA Aircraft Registration Branch, Oklahoma City, Oklahoma.

5. INSTRUCTIONS FOR COMPLETING FAA FORM 337. The person who performs or supervises a major repair or major alteration should prepare FAA Form 337. The form is executed at least in duplicate and is used to record major repairs and major alterations made to an aircraft, spare part, or spare appliance. The following instructions apply to corresponding items 1 through 8 of the form as illustrated in Appendix 1.

a. Item 1 - Aircraft. Information to complete the "Make," "Model," and "Serial Number" blocks will be found on the aircraft manufacturer's identification plate. The "Nationality and Registration Mark" is the same as shown on the Certificate of Aircraft Registration, AC Form 8050-3.

Initiated by: AWS-340

b. Item 2 - Owner. Enter the aircraft owner's complete name and address as shown on the Certificate of Aircraft Registration.

Note: When a major repair or alteration is made to a spare part or appliance, items 1 and 2 will be left blank and the original and duplicate copy of the form will remain with the part until such time as it is installed on an aircraft. The person installing the part will then enter the required information in blocks 1 and 2; give the original of the form to the aircraft owner/operator and forward the duplicate copy to the local FAA District Office.

c. Item 3 - for FAA Use Only. When the FAA determines that the data used in performing a major repair or major alteration complies with accepted industry practices, an appropriate approval statement will be entered here. This block is used when the repair or alteration data has not been previously approved by the FAA. See paragraph 6b for further details.

d. Item 4 - Unit Identification. The information blocks under item 4 are used to identify the airframe, powerplant, propeller, or appliance repaired or altered. It is only necessary to complete the blocks for the unit repaired or altered.

e. Item 5 - Type. Enter a checkmark in the appropriate column to indicate if the unit was repaired or altered.

f. Item 6 - Conformity Statement.

(1) "A" - Agency's Name and Address: Enter name of the mechanic, repair station, or manufacturer accomplishing the repair or alteration. Mechanics should enter their name and permanent mailing address. Manufacturers and repair stations should enter the name and address under which they do business.

(2) "B" - Kind of Agency: Check the appropriate box to indicate the type of person or organization who performed the work.

(3) "C" - Certificate Number: Mechanics should enter their mechanic certificate number in this block, e.g., 1305888. Repair stations should enter their air agency certificate number and the rating or ratings under which the work was performed, e.g., 1234, Airframe Class 3. Manufacturers should enter their type and/or production certificate number. Manufacturers altering TSO appliances should enter the TSO number of the appliance altered.

(4) "D" - Compliance Statement. This space is used to certify that the repair or alteration was made in accordance with Federal Aviation Regulations. When work was performed or supervised by certificated

mechanics not employed by a manufacturer or repair station, they should enter the date the repair or alteration was completed and sign their full name. Repair stations are permitted to authorize persons in their employ to date and sign this conformity statement.

g. Item 7 - Approval for Return to Service. Federal Aviation Regulations, Part 43, establishes the conditions under which major repairs or alterations to airframes, powerplants, propellers, and/or appliances may be approved for return to service. This portion of the form is used to indicate approval or rejection of the repair or alteration of the unit involved and to identify the person or agency making the airworthiness inspection. Check the "approved" or "rejected" box to indicate the finding. Additionally, check the appropriate box to indicate who made the finding. Use the box labeled "other" to indicate a finding by a person other than those listed. Enter the date the finding was made. The authorized person who made the finding should sign the form and enter the appropriate certificate or designation number.

h. Item 8 - Description of Work Accomplished. A clear, concise, and legible statement describing the work accomplished should be entered in item 8 on the reverse side of FAA Form 337. It is important that the location of the repair or alteration, relative to the aircraft or component, be described.

(1) For example, if a repair was made to a buckled spar, the description entered in this part might begin by stating, "Removed wing from aircraft and removed skin from outer 6 feet. Repaired buckled spar 49" from tip in accordance with . . . ." and continue with a description of the repair. The description should refer to applicable FAR Sections and to the use of FAA approved data necessary to substantiate the airworthiness of the repair or alteration. If the repair or alteration is subject to being covered by skin or other structure, a statement should be made certifying a precover inspection was made and found satisfactory.

(2) Data which may be used as a basis for approval of major repairs or alterations includes: FAR (e.g., airworthiness directives), AC's (e.g., AC 43.13-1A), technical standard orders (TSO's), parts manufacturing approval (PMA), FAA approved manufacturer's instructions, kits and service handbooks, type certificate data sheets, and aircraft specifications. Other forms of approved data would be those approved by a designated engineering representative (DER), a manufacturer holding a delegation option authorization (DOA), supplemental type certificates (STC's), and reference to previous FAA field approvals. Supporting data such as stress analyses, test reports, sketches, or photographs should be submitted with the FAA Form 337. This supporting data will be returned to the applicant by the local FAA district office, as only the FAA Form 337 is retained as a part of the aircraft records at Oklahoma City.

(3) If additional space is needed to describe the repair or alteration, attach sheets bearing the aircraft nationality and registration mark and the date work was completed.

(4) It is not required to show weight and balance computations under this item; however, it may be done. In all cases where weight and balance of the aircraft are affected, the changes should be entered in the aircraft weight and balance records with the date, signature, and reference to the FAA Form 337 that instituted the changes.

6. ADMINISTRATIVE PROCESSING. At least an original and one duplicate copy of the FAA Form 337 will be executed. FAA district office processing of the forms and their supporting data will depend upon whether previously approved or non-previously approved data was used as follows:

a. Previously Approved Data. The applicant will complete the forms as instructed in this AC ensuring that item 7, "Approval for Return to Service," has been properly executed; give the original of the form to the aircraft owner or operator, and send the duplicate copy to the local FAA district office.

b. Non-previously Approved Data. The applicant will complete the forms as instructed in this AC leaving item 7, "Approval for Return to Service," blank. Both copies of the form, with supporting data, will be sent to the local FAA district office. When the FAA determines that the major repair or alteration data complies with applicable regulations and is in conformity with accepted industry practices, data approval will be recorded by entering an appropriate statement in item 3, "For FAA Use Only." Both forms and supporting data will be returned to the applicant who will complete item 7, "Approval for Return to Service." The applicant will give the original of the form, with its supporting data, to the aircraft owner or operator and return the duplicate copy to the local FAA district office who will, in turn, forward it to the FAA Aircraft Registration Branch, Oklahoma City, Oklahoma, for inclusion in the aircraft records.

M. C. BEARD
Acting Director
Office of Airworthiness

APPENDIX 1. FAA FORM 337 (FRONT), MAJOR REPAIR AND ALTERATION (AIRFRAME, POWERPLANT, PROPELLER, OR APPLIANCE)

DEPARTMENT OF TRANSPORTATION
FEDERAL AVIATION ADMINISTRATION

MAJOR REPAIR AND ALTERATION
(Airframe, Powerplant, Propeller, or Appliance)

Form Approved
OMB No. 04-R0060

FOR FAA USE ONLY
OFFICE IDENTIFICATION

INSTRUCTIONS: Print or type all entries. See FAR 43.9, FAR 43 Appendix B, and AC 43.9-1 (or subsequent revision thereof) for instructions and disposition of this form. This report is required by law (49 U.S.C. 1421). Failure to report can result in a civil penalty of not to exceed $1,000 for each such violation (Section 901 Federal Aviation Act of 1958).

1. AIRCRAFT	MAKE ROBIN	MODEL RA-15-150
	SERIAL NO. 15-10521	NATIONALITY AND REGISTRATION MARK N-3763
2. OWNER	NAME (As shown on registration certificate) William Taylor	ADDRESS (As shown on registration certificate) 36 Main Street Cambria, Pennsylvania 15946

3. FOR FAA USE ONLY

The data identified herein complies with the applicable airworthiness requirements and is approved for the above described aircraft, subject to conformity inspection by a person authorized by FAR Part 43, Section 43.7.

AEA-GADO-19	April 5, 1979	Ralph Burlingame (signed) Ralph Burlingame
District Office	DATE	Signature of FAA Inspector

4. UNIT IDENTIFICATION				5. TYPE	
UNIT	MAKE	MODEL	SERIAL NO.	REPAIR	ALTERATION
AIRFRAME	********************* (As described in item 1 above) *********************			X	
POWERPLANT					
PROPELLER					
APPLIANCE	TYPE MANUFACTURER				

6. CONFORMITY STATEMENT

A. AGENCY'S NAME AND ADDRESS	B. KIND OF AGENCY	C. CERTIFICATE NO.
George Morris High Streeet Johnstown, Pennsylvania 15236	X U.S. CERTIFICATED MECHANIC FOREIGN CERTIFICATED MECHANIC CERTIFICATED REPAIR STATION MANUFACTURER	1305888

D. I certify that the repair and/or alteration made to the unit(s) identified in item 4 above and described on the reverse or attachments hereto have been made in accordance with the requirements of Part 43 of the U.S. Federal Aviation Regulations and that the information furnished herein is true and correct to the best of my knowledge.

DATE	SIGNATURE OF AUTHORIZED INDIVIDUAL
March 19, 1979	George Morris (signed) George Morris

7. APPROVAL FOR RETURN TO SERVICE

Pursuant to the authority given persons specified below, the unit identified in item 4 was inspected in the manner prescribed by the Administrator of the Federal Aviation Administration and is [X] APPROVED [ ] REJECTED

BY					OTHER (Specify)
	FAA FLT. STANDARDS INSPECTOR	MANUFACTURER	X	INSPECTION AUTHORIZATION	
	FAA DESIGNEE	REPAIR STATION		CANADIAN DEPARTMENT OF TRANSPORT INSPECTOR OF AIRCRAFT	

DATE OF APPROVAL OR REJECTION	CERTIFICATE OR DESIGNATION NO.	SIGNATURE OF AUTHORIZED INDIVIDUAL
April 9, 1979	237412	Donald Pauley (signed) Donald Pauley

FAA Form 337 (8320)

FAA FORM 337 (BACK), MAJOR REPAIR AND ALTERATION (AIRFRAME, POWERPLANT, PROPELLER, OR APPLIANCE)

NOTICE

Weight and balance or operating limitation changes shall be entered in the appropriate aircraft record. An alteration must be compatible with all previous alterations to assure continued conformity with the applicable airworthiness requirements.

8. DESCRIPTION OF WORK ACCOMPLISHED *(If more space is required, attach additional sheets. Identify with aircraft nationality and registration mark and date work completed.)*

1. Removed right wing from aircraft and removed skin from outer 6 feet. Repaired buckled spar 49" from tip in accordance with attached photographs and figure 1 of drawing dated March 6, 1979.

   DATE: March 14, 1979, inspected splice in Item 1 and found it to be in accordance with data indicated. Splice is okay to cover. Inspected internal and external wing assembly for hidden damage and condition.

   Donald Pauley, IA 237412

2. Primed interior wing structure and replaced skin P/Ns 63-0085, 63-0086, 63-00878 with same material, 2024T3, .025" thick. Rivet size and spacing all the same as original and using procedures in Chapter 2, Section 3 of AC 43.13-1A, dated 1972.

3. Replaced stringers as required and installed 6 splices as per attached drawing and photographs.

4. Installed wing, rigged aileron, and operationally checked in accordance with manufacturers maintenance manual.

5. No change in weight or balance.

END

☐ ADDITIONAL SHEETS ARE ATTACHED

2 U.S. GOVERNMENT PRINTING OFFICE: 1979-251-568/230

AC NO: 43-5

DATE: 8/13/74

ADVISORY CIRCULAR

DEPARTMENT OF TRANSPORTATION
FEDERAL AVIATION ADMINISTRATION

SUBJECT: AIRWORTHINESS DIRECTIVES FOR GENERAL AVIATION AIRCRAFT

1. PURPOSE.

The purposes of this Advisory Circular are to point out areas of misunderstanding regarding:

a. Aircraft owners and operators' responsibility for complying with Airworthiness Directives.

b. Maintenance personnel responsibilities with regards to performance of Airworthiness Directives.

c. Maintenance record entries for AD's required by FAR 91.173(a)(2)(v) and FAR 43.9.

2. REFERENCE.

FAR Part 39, Airworthiness Directives.

3. BACKGROUND.

When an aeronautical product is new, engineers have to rely on past history of similar products or analyses to predict when defects or unsafe conditions will arise when service time is accumulated. As service time is accumulated, various problems can arise that create unsafe conditions and the conditions could exist in other products of the same type design. This happens even though the manufacturers conduct extensive testing under all types of simulated and real conditions. When an unsafe condition is discovered, the owners or operators of the product are notified of the unsafe condition and the corrective action that must be taken, inspections that must be made or conditions and limitations under which the product may be operated.

4. NOTIFICATION.

Airworthiness Directives are Federal Aviation Regulations (FARs). They are published in the Federal Register as amendments to FAR Part 39. In some instances, they are published as a Notice of Proposed Rulemaking and the public is invited to comment on the contents. In other instances they are published as adopted rules. This is done when immediate compliance is necessary to ensure safety of the product concerned. When the comments are received, they are given consideration. If any changes are considered necessary as a result of the review, they are made. After such changes, or if no changes are considered necessary, the AD is again published in the Federal Register as an adopted rule with a compliance date included. It is also possible that after the NPRM is issued, the FAA will find that the AD is unnecessary and withdraw the AD.

When an AD becomes an adopted rule, it is printed and mailed to the registered owner, in the event that the AD applies to an aircraft. If the AD is on an engine, propeller, accessory, or appliance, and it can be determined which aircraft models are affected, the AD is also mailed to the registered owner. However, there are many times when the specific make and model cannot be determined. The AD is then printed and included in a biweekly summary of all ADs that have been adopted in the preceding two weeks. This biweekly summary is sent to all subscribers to the AD summary which is for sale by (ref. AC 39-6D):

Department of Transportation
Federal Aviation Administration
Aeronautical Center, Attention: AAC-23
P.O. Box 25461
Oklahoma City, Oklahoma 73125

5. EMERGENCY ADs.

There are times when an unsafe condition arises that is of such seriousness as to require immediate corrective action. In these cases, an Emergency AD is processed and notification is made in one of two ways. The first, in the case of nontransport aircraft, when there are numerous aircraft involved, is by an Air Mail letter to each registered owner of the aircraft involved. In the second instance, for transport aircraft, when there are relatively few aircraft involved, notification is made by telegram. Emergency ADs are usually not adopted rules to Part 39; therefore, no AD number (or amendment number) has been assigned. In all cases, however, they will subsequently be processed and published as an adopted rule.

Emergency ADs have relatively short compliance times; in many instances they must be complied with before further flight of the aircraft involved and are effective upon receipt. This creates a problem in the case of leased aircraft, for it is important that the registered owner make the information available to the operators of the aircraft in the most expeditious manner possible because FAA has no other means available to make notification other than to the registered owner. Unless the registered owner makes the information available to the lessee, the lessee may not be aware of a serious condition.

6. COMPLIANCE.

Since the ADs are printed as an amendment to FAR Part 39, and they are published in the Federal Register, they meet the requirements of the Administrative Procedure, Title 5 U.S.C. 552 et seq., in that they are a Federal Aviation Regulation and must be complied with the same as any other regulation. This means that no person may operate a product to which an AD applies, unless it is operated in accordance with the limitations established in the AD. In this context, the definition of "operate" in FAR Part 1, should be studied. It will be seen that operate not only means the person who uses, but applies to the person who causes the product to be used or authorizes it to be used. In addition, FAR Section 91.163 places the responsibility for the airworthiness of an aircraft upon the owner or operator. If the provisions of the AD have not been complied with, the aircraft cannot be considered to be in airworthy condition.

7. COMPLIANCE DATES.

a. *One Time Compliances:* There are various compliance dates used in preparing ADs due to the differences in the nature of the unsafe condition. Some ADs must be complied with before further flight due to the seriousness of the unsafe condition and the expected frequency of occurrences in other like make and models. There are others that are not required to be complied with until some specified time in the future, when it has been determined that immediate action is not necessary. This is not meant to minimize the seriousness of the unsafe condition, but rather to provide a reasonable time for compliance.

All AD compliances are not specified in periods of time. Some compliance frequencies are listed by number of cycles, landings, or other specified types of operations. These compliances are necessary since calendar time or time in service alone does not increase the unsafe condition. As an example, an unsafe condition on a landing gear would become more critical due to takeoffs and landings rather than time in service or calendar time.

b. *Repetitive Compliances:* Not all ADs are written with a one-time compliance. Many have recurring or repetitive compliances due to the nature of the unsafe condition. In these cases, the importance of the maintenance records (FAR 91.173) cannot be overemphasized. This will be further discussed in Item 9 below. The message in this section is to ascertain if an AD must be complied with again at a future date and somehow establish a schedule for its accomplishment. It is the owner or operator's responsibility to see that ADs are complied with (see Par. 8, Responsibility for Compliance) and while arrangements can be made with others, the owner or operator is still the responsible party.

8. RESPONSIBILITY FOR COMPLIANCE.

The basic responsibility for seeing that ADs are complied with rests with the owner or operator. (Ref. FAR 91.163.) Many owner/operators are not fully aware of this and feel that the maintenance personnel should see that the ADs are complied with. It is true that maintenance personnel must ensure that AD notes that are due are complied with when performing the 100 hour, annual or progressive inspections. However, all AD notes may not be due for compliance at this time and may have compliance dates that call for compliance at a later date. In addition, the aircraft may be undergoing an inspection under FAR Section 91.217 and in this case the maintenance personnel are only required to comply with ADs that are related to that portion of the aircraft undergoing inspection. This is true due to the nature of the inspection program not encompassing a complete aircraft inspection at one time. Therefore, it is incumbent upon the owner/operator to ensure that ADs are complied with when due. Again, the importance of maintenance records can be seen. (See Par. 9.)

Once the owner/operator has fulfilled his responsibility by causing the aircraft to be taken into maintenance for compliance with an AD, the performance and recording of the work itself is the responsibility of the maintenance agency involved. However, when the aircraft is approved for return to service, the owner/operator is once more responsible to see that appropriate entries are made in the maintenance records.

9. MAINTENANCE RECORDS (FAR 91.173 and FAR 43.9).

One of the most important items to be considered by the owner/operator is the maintenance records. He is required by regulation to include in them the current status of applicable ADs which will include the method of compliance. This is important because frequently, there is more than one way of complying with an AD. The records also act as your receipt for work accomplished. All too frequently, owner/operators have had ADs complied with a second time because they failed to have the records completed by maintenance personnel.

Another important part that maintenance records can play is to establish when repetitive inspections will be due. A well-established set of records will not only schedule when repetitive ADs are due, but can schedule one time ADs that are due at some future date.

One aspect of maintenance records that has given problems in the past is when engines, propellers, or accessories are sent to FAA Certified Repair Stations for major repairs, including compliance with an AD. Repair stations should be aware that the wording of the maintenance release in Appendix B of FAR 43 does not fully meet the requirement of 43.9 for recording compliance with AD notes. They should furnish a description record as provided in the recording requirements for documenting compliance with Airworthiness Directives. It is then incumbent upon the owner to include this in his maintenance records to comply with FAR 91.173(a)(2)(v), which requires the current status of applicable Airworthiness Directives, including the method of compliance.

10. RESTRICTED CATEGORY AIRCRAFT.

In the past, considerable confusion has existed as to whether ADs applied to Restricted Category aircraft. This has come about, in part, due to the policy in the old Civil Aeronautics Manual 8, Section 8.20–1(b)(2), which stated that ADs did not have to be complied with on Restricted Category aircraft.

To preclude further questions as to whether or not an AD applies to all products of the same type design, future ADs that do not limit their applicability will apply to all models set forth in the AD regardless of category.

CAM 8.20–1(b)(2) is no longer policy. When an AD is encountered which is not clear as to applicability, the specific question or problem should be referred to the local Flight Standards District Office for a determination of applicability.

C. R. MELUGIN, JR.
Acting Director, Flight Standards Service

Glossary

This glossary of terms is provided to serve as a ready reference for the words with which you may not be familiar. These definitions may differ from those of standard dictionaries, but are in keeping with shop usuage.

airworthiness directive A directive issued by the FAA to correct an unsafe condition that may exist on an aircraft and it must be complied with.

airworthy Safe for flight and meets all of the applicable requirements determined by the FAA and the manufacturer to be necessary for flying the aircraft.

annual inspection An inspection designed to determine if an aircraft is airworthy or unairworthy.

appliance Any instrument, mechanism, equipment, part, apparatus, appurtenance, or accessory, including communications equipment, that is used or intended to be used in operating or controlling an aircraft in flight, is installed in or attached to the aircraft, and is not part of an airframe, engine, or propeller.

applicability Something that applies to and/or affects another.

approved This term has two definitions in this publication. One definition is that a mechanic has approved or stated the aircraft has met all applicable airworthiness requirements and is ready for flight. The other definition is that the information is approved by the FAA such as found on the back of the Form 337.

approved inspection system A maintenance program consisting of the inspection and maintenance necessary to maintain an aircraft in airworthy condition.

authorized Being given the legal right to perform certain functions by the FAA.

calendar month A time period that expires on the last day of the month irregardless on what day of the month it begins.

certificate An official FAA document authorizing a privilege, fact, or legal concept.

compliance To accomplish as required by regulation or directive.

conformity Meeting all of the requirements of its original or properly altered conditions as specified in the Type Certificate Data Sheets and the manufacturer's specifications.

continuous airworthiness program A maintenance program consisting of the inspection and maintenance necessary to maintain an aircraft or a fleet of aircraft in airworthy condition and is usually used on large or turbine powered aircraft.

designated Being given the legal right and authority to perform certain specified functions by the FAA.

detailed inspection item An inspection item of a progressive inspection that requires a close and careful inspection, may involve disassembly to inspect and could even be to overhaul a component or part.

ELT The common abbreviation for the emergency locator transmitter.

inspect The determination of the condition of something by sight, feel, measurement, or other methods.

inspection The determination of the condition of something by sight, feel, measurement, or other means.

life-limited part A part or component that has a designated number of hours or calendar time in service after which it will be replaced and is no longer usable.

maintenance release A return to service approval in the appropriate maintenance record.

major alteration A change to an aircraft or its components that might appreciably affect weight, balance, structural strength, performance, powerplant operation, flight characteristics, or other qualities affecting airworthiness, or that is not done according to accepted practices or cannot be done by elementary operations and is not included in the Type Certificate Data Sheets or manufacturer's specification for the aircraft.

major repair A repair that if improperly done, might appreciably affect weight, balance, structural strength, performance, powerplant operation, flight characteristics, or other qualities affecting airworthiness, or that is not done according to accepted practices or cannot be done by elementary operations.

phase A section or a distinguishable part of a maintenance program or inspection.

preventive maintenance Simple or minor preservative operations and the replacement of small standard parts not involving complex assembly operation as listed in Appendix A of FAR 43.

recurring An airworthiness directive that requires compliance at regular hourly or calendar time periods.

return to service The completion of all applicable maintenance records and forms after maintenance has been performed on an aircraft that will allow the aircraft to be legally flown.

routine inspection items Inspection items listed in a progressive inspection that require only a visual inspection to determine their condition.

time-in-service The time from the moment an aircraft leaves the surface of the earth until it touches down at the next point of landing.

Answers to Study Questions

Section I

1. Owner or operator of the aircraft.
2. 12 calendar months.
3. 96 hours.
4. An annual inspection is all that is required.
5. When the aircraft is flown under instrument flight rules.
6. 24 calendar months.
7. 24 calendar months.

Section II

1. An A&P mechanic or an authorized representative of a certified repair station if all the maintenance items repaired are classified as a minor repair.
2. June 30, 1986.
3. Yes.
4. an authorized inspector, an authorized representative of a certificated repair station, and the manufacturer of the aircraft.
5. Those aircraft flown for hire and those that are used for flight instruction for hire in an aircraft that the instructor provides.
6. Yes, but only on a special flight or ferry permit.
7. 10 hours.
8. An A&P mechanic.
9. Less down time at one time for the aircraft.

Section III

1. Own design, manufacturers, another person.
2. Maximum power rpm with the aircraft stationary or not moving.
3. Static and idle rpm, magnetos, fuel and oil pressures, cylinder and oil temperatures, all other operating systems for manfacturer's specifications.
4. Preinspection phase, look phase, service and repair phase, functional check phase, and return to service phase.
5. Look phase.
6. By completing the appropriate entries in the maintenance records.

Section IV

1. Yes.

2. No.

3. Condition, cleanliness, TSO C22 printed on the identification tag, security of attachment, and operation of the latching mechanism.

4. Airworthiness certificate, registration certificate.

5. Proper installation, battery replacement date, antenna connection and condition, and operation.

6. Water level and proper state of charge.

7. Retraction safety switch, excessive wear, proper operation, binding, chafing, uplock operation, electrical switch operation, uplock tension and clearance, up indicating system, gear warning horn operation, downlocks for proper operation and tension, downlock indicating lights and switches, door operation and fit.

8. Oil screen and compression check.

9. Timing, breaker point condition, lubrication, security or mounting, and internal oil leakage.

Section V

1. Owner or operator of the aircraft.

2. Yes.

3. When it has been rebuilt by the manufacturer.

4. The rotor is a life limited part.

5. So you have a separate record for it should you put it on another engine.

6. Total time in service, current status of life limited parts, the time since last overhaul of items required to be overhauled on a time basis, current inspection status of the aircraft, status of applicable airworthiness directives, and a current list of the major alterations.

7. Form 337

8. The owner or operator of the aircraft.

9. One year unless sooner superceded by other work.

Section VI

1. Date, description of the work or reference to data of the repair, name, signature, and certificate number.

2. An authorized representative of the repair station.

3. Date, total time, name of inspection, certification statement, signature, and certificate number.

4. 48 hours.

5. Yes, a 100-hour inspection can be signed off as unairworthy.

6. Date, total time, AD number, AD revision date, method of compliance, next due time or date, name, signature and certificate number.

7. Two.

8. One copy is placed in the owners maintenance record and one copy is sent to the local FAA district office.

Final Examination

STUDENT: ____________________________

GRADE: ________________

Select the best, or correct answer from the choices listed below the questions.

1. Who is primarily responsible for maintaining an aircraft in airworthy condition?

   A. A&P mechanic

   B. Owner or operator

   C. FAA inspector

   D. Authorized inspector.

2. On aircraft requiring an annual inspection how often is this inspection required?

   A. Once a year

   B. 12 months

   C. 24 months

   D. 12 calendar months.

3. How many hours may a 100-hour inspection be exceeded if necessary to fly to a place where the inspection can be performed?

   A. 1 hour

   B. 5 hours

   C. 10 hours

   D. 20 hours.

4. If an annual inspection is completed on June 6, 1985, when will the inspection period expire?

   A. June 6, 1986

   B. June 6, 1988

   C. June 30, 1985

   D. June 30, 1986

5. Who can perform and approve for return to service an annual inspection?

   A. Authorized inspector

   B. A&P mechanic

   C. Owner or operator

   D. Repair station.

6. Who can approve an aircraft for return to service after a 100-hour inspection has been completed?

   A. Repair station

   B. A&P mechanic

   C. Owner or operator

   D. Repairman.

7. What is required to fly an aircraft after the annual inspection has expired to a place where it can be performed?

   A. Nothing is needed as it can be exceeded by 5 hour

   B. Owners permission

   C. An A&P mechanics permission

   D. A special flight or ferry permit from the FAA.

8. What type of inspection is required when an aircraft is placed on a progressive inspection system?

   A. Manufacturers recommended inspection

   B. A phase inspection

   C. Annual inspection

   D. A special FAA inspection.

9. Who must supervise a progressive inspection system on an aircraft?

   A. Owner or operator

   B. Authorized inspector

   C. A&P mechanic

   D. Any repair station.

10. Who can sign off or approve for return to service the various phases of a progressive inspection?

   A. A&P mechanic

   B. Repairman

   C. Any repair station

   D. Owner or operator.

11. Who must select the type of inspection program that is used on a large or turbine powered multi-engine aircraft?

   A. Owner or operator

   B. Authorized inspector

   C. National Transportation Safety Board

   D. FAA.

12. What is issued by the FAA to correct unsafe conditions that may exist in an aircraft?

   A. Service bulletins

   B. Airworthiness directives

   C. Service letters

   D. Technical standard orders.

13. A manufacturer of an aircraft may issue information concerning an improvement or change that may be made on an aircraft, these changes are called

   A. Airworthiness directives

   B. Service bulletins

   C. Technical standard orders

   D. Advisory circulars.

14. When inspecting the seat belts in an aircraft what TSO number should be printed on the identification tag?

   A. TSO C14A

   B. TSO C15C

   C. TSO C22B

   D. TSO C64A

15. What aircraft document must be displayed in the interior of the aircraft?

A. Registration certificate

B. Airworthiness certificate

C. FCC license

D. Weight and balance data.

16. What appendix in FAR Part 43 covers the minimum inspection requirements on an aircraft?

A. Appendix A

B. Appendix B

C. Appendix C

D. Appendix D

17. According to FAR Part 43 what must be used in performing an inspection on an aircraft?

A. A flashlight

B. An inspector mirror

C. A checklist

D. A multimeter.

18. On an aircraft equipped with a retractable landing gear what must be done during the inspection to insure proper operation of the landing gear?

A. Disassemble and overhaul the strut assembly

B. Change fluid in the strut

C. Dye check the retraction links

D. Perform a retraction and extension check.

19. When performing a 100-hour inspection on the engine you are required to

A. Retorque all the cylinder hold down bolts.

B. Perform a compression check

C. Grind the valves

D. Change the spark plugs.

20. Before approving an aircraft for returns to service following a 100-hour inspection you are required to

A. Operate the engine and perform certain functional checks

B. Notify the local FAA office

C. Test fly the aircraft

D. Taxi the aircraft.

21. When inspecting the ELT on an aircraft you should check

A. Date of installation

B. Date of last operational check

C. Date of battery replacement

D. Date of TSO compliance.

22. When performing the operational check on the engine which of the following rpm checks should be done?

A. Idle and cruise rpm

B. Static and cruise rpm

C. Cruise and full power rpm

D. Idle and static rpm.

23. Who if primarily responsible for having and maintaining the aircraft maintenance records?

A. A&P mechanic performing the work on the aircraft

B. Owner or operator of the aircraft

C. FAA

D. An authorized inspector.

24. Who is responsible for making appropriate entries in the maintenance records after performing an inspection or maintenance on the aircraft?

A. A&P mechanic performing the work on the aircraft

B. Owner or operator of the aircraft

C. FAA

D. Pilot of the aircraft.

25. Which of the following is considered to be a part of the permanent maintenance records on an aircraft?

A. Time in service of the aircraft

B. Record of all annual inspections

C. Record of all service bulletins complied with

D. Record of all 100-hour inspections.

26. How long must the temporary maintenance records be retained?

A. 6 months, unless sooner superceded by other work

B. 9 months, unless sooner superceded by other work

C. 12 months, unless sooner superceded by other work

D. 24 months, unless sooner superceded by other work.

27. The five items required in a maintenance record entry returning a minor repair to service are

A. Date, tach time, description of work, signature, and certificate number

B. Date, total time, description of work, name and certificate number

C. Total time, description of work, signature, and certificate number

D. Date, description of work, a name, signature, and certificate number.

28. The six items required in a maintenance record entry approving a 100-hour inspection for return to service are:

A. Date, total time, type of inspection, certification statement, signature, and certificate number

B. Date, tach time, certification statement, name, signature, and certificate number

C. Date total time, tach time, certification statement, name, and certificate number.

D. Date, tach time, type of inspection, signature, and certificate number.

29. The form used to record and approve for return to service major alterations and repairs is called a Form

A. 802

B. 727

C. 337

D. 2350.

30. The information required in a maintenance record entry for the compliance with a recurring airworthiness directive are:

A. Date, tach time, AD number, signature, and certificate number

B. Date, total time, AD number, revision date, method of compliance, next due time or date, name, signature, and certificate number

C. Date, total time, AD number, method of compliance, signature, certificate number

D. Date, AD number, method of compliance, name, signature, and certificate number.

Final Examination Answers

1. B
2. D
3. C
4. C
5. A
6. B
7. D
8. C
9. B
10. A
11. A
12. B
13. B
14. C
15. B
16. D
17. C
18. D
19. B
20. A
21. C
22. D
23. B
24. A
25. A
26. C
27. D
28. A
29. C
30. B

NOTES:

NOTES:

NOTES: